The Power
of the Point
# of Contact

Dr. Morris Cerullo

Published by:

MORRIS CERULLO WORLD EVANGELISM

P.O. Box 85277 • San Diego, CA 92186
(858) 277-2200

E-mail: morriscerullo@mcwe.com
Website: www.mcwe.com

For prayer 24 hours a day, 7 days a week, call: **1(858)HELPLINE**
435-7546
HELPLINE FAX 1-858-427-0555

INTERNATIONAL LINE: 001-858 HELPLINE

MORRIS CERULLO WORLD EVANGELISM OF CANADA

P.O. Box 3600 • Concord, Ontario, L4K-1B6
(905) 669-1788

MORRIS CERULLO WORLD EVANGELISM OF GREAT BRITAIN

P.O. Box 277 • Hemel Hempstead, HERTS HP2-7DH
44 (0)1 442 232432

Dedication

There has been so much said about the wives of authors in dedications. Knowing and feeling that this book, *The Power of the Point of Contact* would be one of the most Spirit-led that God would have me author, I began to pray. Who was worthy enough for me to honor that would make the dedication real, and not just words.

With this awesome sense, I hereby dedicate without reservation, or hesitation, this book to a WOMAN of faith, love, and power. A woman who is so deeply loved around the world; that millions from every nation in the world call her "Mama."

Yes, it is true they take her into their heart by millions in Africa, Japan, Korea, the Philippines, Hong Kong, Malaysia, Singapore, Indonesia, and all of North, Central and South America, for she has sacrificed her husband to the Kingdom.

This Proverbs 31 woman, is none other than Mrs. Theresa Cerullo, who at this time of dedication is my faithful wife of 51 years.

Yes, Solomon, "Who can find a virtuous woman? Her price is far above rubies. The heart of her husband does safely trust in her, so that he shall have no need of spoil." Proverbs 31:10-11

ISAIAH 41:10

Introduction

Faith is the key to touching God and getting your prayers answered. Without faith, prayers are simply words spoken into the wind, forever going nowhere. Rudderless boats adrift on the sea of time.

It is interesting to note the things that do not move the hand of God. Sickness, sorrow, suffering, sadness, heartache, pain, lack, want, poverty, divorce and grief, to name just a few, have yet to cause God to spring into action.

This is not to say that our Lord is not concerned with these problems. He is! But...none of these things in and of themselves cause God to act. If these or any other maladies troubling the human race moved His hand, the problem would cease to be.

Is there a formula, a code, a method that assures men and women success each time they approach God? Is there something we can do or say that will capture His attention and cause His voice to thunder from the Heavens?

No! And the reason is God wants you and me to approach Him in faith, not by some methodology designed by men.

Several years ago I read a story about a scientific study done with pigeons. A timer was set to drop seed into each cage at pre-determined times.

The next day when the scientist returned to observe the birds he was amused to find each doing something totally different.

One pigeon would lower one wing and dance in a circle until the seed fell into the tray. He would stop dancing, eat and start the routine all over again until once again the seed appeared in the tray.

Each bird had its own individual procedure it went through as if what he was doing caused the seed to fall into the tray.

I'm convinced religion has done the same thing!

God raised up a group of special men in the 1940's, Oral Roberts, Billy Graham, William Branham, Jack Coe, T. L. Osborn, A. A. Allen, Velmer Gardner and myself. We were anointed and sent out to spearhead a great revival across America and around the world.

Without exception, we were each led to sanctify a fast to the Lord. For some of us, the time of fasting and prayer lasted forty days. At the end of our fast we emerged from our prayer closet charged with the power to work the works of Christ.

When miracles started accompanying our ministry some wonderful men and women of God thought fasting was the key to receiving a powerful ministry, so they too fasted.

Each ministry was blessed and enhanced, but fasting, of itself, was not the key to receiving a miracle-producing ministry. One well-meaning pastor in Texas fasted so long that he injured his health. He was looking for a method that does not exist.

In this book you will discover the glorious truth that your "Point of Contact" may be different from that of any other person in the world. You are an individual, uniquely designed of God. He wants you to be blessed and the desires of your heart to be fulfilled.

Get ready for the most exciting journey of your life as you read, *The Power of the Point of Contact!*

Section One

The Point of Contact for Healing

Section Two

The Point of Contact for Personal Direction

Section Three

The Point of Contact for Prosperity

Section Four

The most Powerful Point of Contact in the Universe

Section One

Introduction

Modern religious philosophy would have you think the devil is simply a figment of the imagination. That's where man-made religion and the Word of God are diametrically opposed.

This is what the Bible says:

> *Be sober, be vigilant; because your adversary the devil, as a roaring lion, walketh about, seeking whom he may devour: Whom resist steadfast in the faith...*

I PETER 5:8-9

In each section of this book you will discover truths that will help you in your personal fight against the forces of darkness.

It is to your advantage to remember that you are in a life and death struggle. The good part is that you are not alone. God has placed within you a magnificent ingredient called faith.

By using the faith He gave you, you can turn the tide against your enemy and live in peace and victory every minute of every day.

Each chapter in this section is dedicated to helping you establish a "Point of Contact" to release your faith for physical healing for yourself or someone you love.

Section One

Chapter 1

"If I May Touch But His Clothes"

Hearing the good news that Jesus was coming her way opened the door to the greatest possibilities her heart could ever desire. It was the opportunity she had been hoping for. Now she would be delivered from a debilitating sickness that made every day a living hell.

For twelve years her life had been reduced to a series of disappointing failures that drained both her strength and her resources. One doctor after another treated her, but rather than getting better the condition continually grew worse.

This pathetic story was the reversal of the famed, "Rags to Riches." The woman had gone from "Riches to Rags!" And... there was no end in sight to the tragic dilemma until she heard the wonderful news that Jesus was in town and that He would be passing not far from her house.

Based on the things she had heard about Him, her condition would not be too hard for the young, miracle-working rabbi called Jesus, even though it was incurable by the physicians of that time!

First of all, she needed a strategy. She couldn't simply walk up to Him and say, "Hello, my name is Mary, (or whatever her name was), and I need a miracle touch."

11

This woman had an issue of blood and the law declared her unclean! The garments she wore, the bed she slept on, the chairs in her house, in-fact, everything in her house and everything she touched purposely or by accident was considered unclean.

Whenever she ventured outside her house she was to call out, "UNCLEAN! UNCLEAN!" lest anyone should touch her and also become unclean. She was an alien among her own people. For all intents and purposes she was dead...while living.

How could she approach this wonderful, miracle-working rabbi given that the Law of Moses prevented her from touching Him or Him from touching her? The law must be obeyed even though its letter stung like the tip of a whip.

It's no wonder that Paul felt compelled in his spirit to write:

> *[It is He] Who has qualified us [making us to be fit and worthy and sufficient] as ministers and dispensers of a new covenant [of salvation through Christ], not [ministers] of the letter (of legally written code) but of the Spirit; for the code [of the Law] kills, but the [Holy] Spirit makes alive.*
>
> II Corinthians 3:6

The Law stood as an impenetrable barrier, but faith looked beyond the Law! The Law had the smell of death written all over it, but faith was bursting forth with new life! The Law said there was no way, but faith dared to rush in where angels fear to tread.

Her religion taught her that God was more concerned with ceremony than He was with people. She was to go through the motions of being religious, but to never expect Jehovah, the God of Abraham, Isaac and Jacob, to actually move on her behalf.

Even though the woman had tried them all, neither

12

religion, the rabbis or the physicians had produced a cure for her. It was evident that the sickness eating away at her body and the constant oozing of blood demanded a radical departure from the normal religious procedure.

She didn't need another doctor's apology or another rabbi reading from the law in the local synagogue...she needed a miracle touch from God that would set her free from the clutches of her twelve year illness!

It was certain, if she had done nothing different, that's exactly what she would have gotten...NOTHING DIFFERENT!

Look at this statement, *"If you continue to do the things you have always done, the way you have always done them and expect different results, you're a fool!"*

Never has that statement been more apropos than in the life of the woman with the issue of blood.

She had literally tried everything and nothing worked. So, it was time to throw caution to the wind, step out in faith and get a miracle from God.

The woman established a "Point of Contact!"

To help you better understand what I mean by my statement a "Point of Contact," let's look at this woman's story in the Bible:

> *And a certain woman, which had an issue of blood twelve years, And had suffered many things of many physicians, and had spent all that she had, and was nothing bettered, but rather grew worse, When she had heard of Jesus, came in the press behind, and touched his garment. For she said, If I may touch but his clothes, I shall be whole. And straightway the fountain of her blood was dried up; and she felt in her body that she was healed of that plague. And Jesus, immediately knowing in himself that virtue had gone out of him,*

turned him about in the press, and said, Who touched my clothes? And his disciples said unto him, Thou seest the multitude thronging thee, and sayest thou, Who touched me? And he looked round about to see her that had done this thing. But the woman fearing and trembling, knowing what was done in her, came and fell down before him, and told him all the truth. And he said unto her, Daughter, thy faith hath made thee whole; go in peace, and be whole of thy plague.

MARK 5:25-34

Establishing a "Point of Contact" must always be the first priority for anyone who needs a miracle from God.

The woman with the issue of blood made the hem of Christ's garment, or as some theologians believe, the fringe of His prayer shawl, the point where her faith would rendezvous with God. It was as if she set an appointment to meet Him at that certain place.

I find it most interesting to note that God was on time to meet her at her pre-selected place. What this means is that your faith actually moves God and creates miracles on your behalf.

There are so many elements in this remarkable account that verify how powerful faith is when it has a "Point of Contact" from which to work.

First of all we should recognize that Jesus was on a special mission to raise a young girl from the dead, (I'll cover that miracle in the next chapter...don't miss it!) when the woman made her daring move. Had she not pressed through the throng and touched Him, Jesus would not have stopped for even a moment. Her act of faith demanded a response from the Master.

This tells me that faith can stop the Lord in His tracks and produce miracles at any given moment if we have established a "Point of Contact".

The second important facet of this story is that faith supercedes the Law. The Law placed stringent limits on men, but faith is limitless.

When I think of faith in action and its limitless power I'm reminded of one of the greatest miracles I have ever witnessed.

I was preaching in the Philippines when all of a sudden I heard the cracking of bones.

Imagine, there were more than thirty thousand people in the meeting and I could hear the sound of bones cracking above the noise of the crowd. I knew exactly where it was coming from.

As I went to the platform that day I saw hundreds of crippled, maimed and blind people in the invalid section. But one man in particular caught my attention. I don't think I have ever seen a more helpless individual anywhere in the world.

His arms and legs were twisted and his deformed body looked as if someone had rolled him into a ball. The moment I heard the cracking of bones I looked directly at him and saw his arms and legs beginning to straighten out. His horribly bent neck and back were jerking wildly as the bones were being retrofitted by the miraculous power of God.

Right before my eyes I saw him stand up straight, every bone in his body, even to his fingers had been made whole. He no longer had a curved spine, twisted arms and legs or gnarled fingers, he was healed...totally healed by the powerful presence of Jesus Christ.

Somewhere in the deep recesses of this man's spirit he had said, "If I can just get to the Morris Cerullo Crusade, God is going to make me whole!" He established a "Point of Contact" for his faith and God met him on the terms of his faith just like He did for the woman with the issue of blood.

The third salient truth in the story of the woman in the Bible is that she made a positive confession concerning her "Point of Contact." Let me stress that this woman was not just hoping or daydreaming, she was speaking:

*For she **said**, If I may touch but his clothes, I shall be whole.*

I especially like this verse in the Amplified Bible!

*For she **kept saying**, If I only touch His garments, I shall be restored to health!*

Notice, "she **kept saying!**"

When you make a positive confession your words are infused with life-giving power and your faith becomes too powerful for the enemy to resist.

This truth is so vitally important that I must not hurry over it, because your confession is the turning point in your life.

If you confess sickness, pain, heartache, problems, hatred, grief or anything else that is negative, your confession takes on a life of its own.

The wise king, Solomon, wrote:

The tongue has the power of life and death, and those who love it will eat its fruit.
PROVERBS 18:21 NIV

I find that same passage in the Living Bible very interesting:

Those who love to talk will suffer the consequences. Men have died for saying the wrong thing.

PROVERBS 18:21TLB

What did that say?

Men have died for saying the wrong thing.

Does the Bible really mean what it says in this verse? Is it possible that with the wrong confession we can actually create an atmosphere of death?

YES! Your confession is so powerful that it can spread death throughout your mind and body with the venom of a cobra or it can burst forth like a life-giving river that blesses, strengthens and heals everything in its path.

Jesus had this to say about our speech:

...The good man out of his good treasure brings forth good, and the evil man out of his evil treasure brings forth evil. I tell you, on the day of judgment men will render account for every careless word they utter; for by your words you will be justified, and by your words you will be condemned.

MATTHEW 12:35-37 RSV

You can't sit around grumbling and complaining and expect good things to happen.

Let me explain it this way!

Your mind doesn't know the difference between fact and fancy, so it responds to what you tell it.

Put this important truth in your spirit... your mind responds to the things you speak, whether the words coming out of your mouth are positive declarations affirming and building up your faith or negative expressions that kill and destroy.

To protect himself from the calamity of his own words the Psalmist David prayed this prayer:

Let the words of my mouth and the meditation of

my heart be acceptable in Your sight, O LORD...

PSALMS 19:14 NKJ

You alone are responsible for the things that come out of your mouth, that's why it is so crucial that you fill your heart and mind with the Written and the Rhema, Word of God!

Jesus said:

...out of the abundance of the heart the mouth speaks.

MATTHEW 12:34

The woman with the issue of blood didn't just say it once and forget about it, she said it and kept on saying, *"If I may touch but his clothes, I shall be whole."* Her confession became her declaration of faith that moved her through the crowd and within arms length of the Great Physician.

I find it interesting that she didn't demand a face-to-face meeting with Him; she was willing to come from behind and touch His garment.

Think for a moment of the many sick people in the crowd that day who were as close or even closer than she was, but they received no miracle.

It wasn't that Jesus lacked the power or was incapable of making each of them whole, on several occasions He delivered entire multitudes. The reason they were not healed was that they failed to approach Him with faith. Spectators, gawkers and onlookers are scarcely ever the recipients of miracles.

It is evident the woman with the issue of blood was more than a spectator; she had a purpose, a plan, a design and an objective. This woman was driven by a living faith that would not take "no," for an answer.

By establishing a "Point of Contact" she had, in effect, set an appointment with divine destiny, she had created an anointed moment that, if need be, could have called the universe to a screeching halt.

Everything in her being resonated with expectation as she watched the crowd approach, for she knew that in the midst of the throng there was a Man who possessed life and freely gave it to anyone who asked.

This Man, Jesus, was the fulfillment of the Prophet Jeremiah's beautiful acclamation:

Ah Lord GOD! Behold, Thou hast made the heavens and the earth by Thy great power and by Thine outstretched arm! Nothing is too difficult for Thee.

JEREMIAH 32:17 NAS

While her illness had proven the ineptness of the rabbis and baffled the physicians, it would be no match for Him who created the ends of the earth. Resident in this Man was the power to make her whole.

Suddenly...as if propelled by an unseen hand, or a power too great to resist, she pushed through the crowd. There He was, so close that all she had to do was reach out and touch His clothes.

Wait! The enemy screamed! You are unclean! You're contaminated! You're undeserving! You're a failure! You're unworthy! He's the Son of God! You can't touch Him with your dirty hands!

How do I know the devil screamed those terrible accusations at her? Because that's what he does to anyone who is on the verge of a miracle. Those are the tactics he has always used. If you allow him, he will convince you that you are not worthy of any of God's blessings.

The truth is...miracles are not the result of any person

19

being worthy, rather, that by faith you have dared to press your way through the forces of darkness and touched God.

The crowning moment of divine destiny she had waited for was before her. The miracle she so badly needed was at her fingertips. The miracle was hers for the taking!

In a split second the years of suffering would all be over. The agony, the shame, the disappointment that had nagged at her spirit, eaten away at her finances and destroyed her self esteem would be forever locked in the pages of the past.

For her this was not a chance meeting with fate, nor was it that her astrological signs were in line.

Nothing could be farther from the truth than to think that it was a mere coincidence, that all of a sudden she found herself on the brink of a miracle.

This woman established a "Point of Contact", a flash, a brief respite where time is bathed in eternity, where the "im" is erased from "impossible", making it **"POSSIBLE"** for the glory of God to flow unabated into the believer's heart.

Without hesitation she reached out and touched the hem of His garment!

At that precise moment the heavenly electrical current was connected to her body. High voltage, healing power flowed from her fingers, throughout her illness weakened body directly to the bleeding tumor or whatever was causing the issue of blood.

Immediately, the pain, the suffering, the physical drain was gone and she felt in her body that she was healed.

Not being one to draw attention to herself, the woman would have happily withdrawn from the crowd, gone her way and blessed the God of Abraham, Isaac and Jacob for sending the Prophet to heal her.

But it didn't happen that way. No sooner had she felt the warm glow of healing power flow through her body than she heard Him say... *"Who touched me?"* Then His eyes, those tender loving eyes, met hers and she knew that He knew, she was the one.

What would happen now, would this young rabbi scold or berate her for breaking the Law of Moses? Would He shame her for willfully disobeying the traditions handed down from the fathers? Would she see a side of Him that no one had ever seen?

Notice what the Word says:

But the woman fearing and trembling, knowing what was done in her, came and fell down before him, and told him all the truth.

There are three words I especially want you to see:

"Fearing, trembling, knowing." She trembled with fear, because she didn't know what to expect from the Lord.

Remember the religious leaders of her day were ruthless and vindictive. They had no regard for the sick and afflicted, and even less if the one who needed help happened to be a woman.

But there is one more word that described her emotions at that particular moment, *"knowing!"* Regardless of what the rabbis or the religious leaders said or thought, she knew what had taken place in her body when she touched His garment.

Nothing could reverse the glorious virtue that flowed from Him to her or take away the healing she had received.

Kneeling before Him, she told Him of the twelve years of suffering, the money she spent on physicians and that it was all to no avail, because the doctors could not help her.

Oh, what gentleness, what kindness and love she saw as she looked into the eyes of the Master. There were no harsh words for her failure to cry out the mandatory warning, no stinging rebuke for breaking the Law. Instead, He spoke to her with tenderness.

Just as the power of God emanating from Him had driven sickness from her body, His words of love and comfort drove fear from her heart.

Hear His voice as He speaks to her, *"Daughter, thy faith hath made thee whole; go in peace, and be whole of thy plague."*

It is so easy to get caught up in the ecstasy of the moment that you lose sight of the one thing that brought all the components of the miracle together...faith!

Jesus dispelled any notion that His garment had healing power when He said, *"Daughter, **thy faith** hath made thee whole."*

Even though He was, in all probability, wearing a prayer shawl, it was not the prayer shawl or any other garment that made her whole, nor was it the touch, it was her faith!

Every child of God needs to be aware of this truth...nothing moves the hand of God except faith!

The Lord does not react to sickness, pain, sadness, poverty, want, lack, depression or any other malady. If He did, those conditions would no longer exist.

God set "faith" as the standard for receiving miracles. Not only did He set the standard, He also gave us the one precious ingredient we need to make it all happen...faith.

Paul made it clear that no one was left out when he wrote:

> *...according as God hath dealt to every man the measure of faith.*
>
> ROMANS 12:3

The apostle was not speaking of the male gender when he

said, *"to every man,"* so the promise is to everyone who names the name of Christ.

You have been given a "measure of faith," now use it to touch God and receive the things you need from Him.

Nothing is more crucial to releasing your faith than establishing a "Point of Contact." For the woman with the issue of blood, it was the hem of Jesus' garment.

In the following chapters of this book you will see how men and women from various walks of life have established their own individual points of contact and as a result have brought the glory of God into their life. You can do the same!

Modern religion would have you believe the Lord is so busy with the big things in the universe that you are of little or no consequence to Him. Don't believe it! God is concerned about you!

The Lord has a miracle with your name on it…all you need to do is establish a "Point of Contact" where you can release your God-given faith and you will have it.

Your "Point of Contact" obviously cannot be to touch the hem of Christ's garment as the woman did two thousand years ago but, it can be the moment the prophet of God anoints you with oil and prays for you.

Just as the woman in the Bible established her "Point of Contact", you can establish yours. Once you do…get ready, because God will meet you and the miracle will be yours.

One thing about this particular story intrigues me. It is the importance of telling others what God has done in your life. I can't overstress how vital this is.

You must never underestimate the influence of your own personal testimony, it is the strongest message some people will ever see or hear.

One of the things that has helped me to reach millions of souls throughout the earth is the faithfulness of men and women to go to their friends and relatives and tell what God did for them in a Morris Cerullo Crusade.

I still hear from people years later telling me how God healed them of blindness, cancer, tumors, paralysis, deafness and even of leprosy. Many of these same individuals have gone on to become pastors, teachers and evangelists. They are doing great things for God simply by telling what God did for them in a Morris Cerullo meeting or crusade.

The woman with the issue of blood established her "Point of Contact" solely on what she had heard. The Bible very clearly says, *"She had heard all about the wonderful miracles Jesus did."* Mark 5:27 TLB

The last recorded interaction this lady had with Christ was when He said to her, *"go in peace, and be whole of thy plague."*

However, that's not the last we hear of her. I want you to read some other verses and I'll let you draw your own conclusion as to whether or not the woman with the issue of blood was returning the favor to others by "telling" her testimony.

Jesus had made a complete circuit; He first crossed the Sea of Galilee and landed at Gennesaret. That's where He delivered the man possessed by a legion of demons.

Having been asked by the people of that region to leave He crossed back over the sea where He was met by Jairus, and going to his home healed the woman with the issue of blood.

Upon His return to Gennesaret, this is what the Scripture says happened:

The news of their arrival spread quickly throughout the city, and soon people were rushing around, telling everyone to bring in their sick to be healed. The sick begged him to let them touch even the tassel of his

robe, and all who did were healed.

MATTHEW 14:35-36 TLB

I want you to especially notice five words in verse 36, *"The sick begged him to let them touch even **the tassel of his robe,** and all who did were healed."*

To see if it is by coincidence that they are asking to touch, "the tassel of his robe," or if it has direct correlation to the woman who had the issue of blood, let's look at Matthew's account of her miracle:

*a woman who had been sick for twelve years with internal bleeding came up behind him and touched **a tassel of his robe.***

MATTHEW 9:20 TLB

The similarities of the woman's statement and that of the multitude are too great for this to be coincidental! I believe the woman who had been healed of the issue of blood was so overjoyed, so happy, so filled with gratitude that she told her story to everyone she could find.

She even became a missionary and crossed the sea to tell others of the great thing Christ had done for her.

That's the power of a testimony!

Not only did she establish a personal "Point of Contact," her testimony was so vibrant and full of life that it inspired others to use the same thing as their "Point of Contact" to release their faith for a miracle.

When Jesus told her to, *"Go in peace,"* she became an ambassador for the Prince of Peace and taught...

"The Power of the Point of Contact"

Section One

Chapter 2
She Shall Live

Scarcely had the boat reached the shore than a multitude gathered to welcome Him. Jairus one of the rulers, or rabbis of the local synagogue, emerged from the crowd, bowed humbly at the feet of the Lord and pled:

> *My little daughter lieth at the point of death: I pray thee, come and lay thy hands on her, that she may be healed; and she shall live.*
>
> MARK 5:23 KJV

It is very easy to ascertain what this rabbi had established as his "Point of Contact." To him the miracle would happen the moment Jesus laid hands on his sick child.

This story exemplifies perfectly that everyone is given the right to establish his or her own personal "Point of Contact." You do not have to follow in someone else's footsteps. There are no set rules that you must adhere to.

As you continue to read this book you will find that individuals in the Bible established several "Points of Contact" for receiving the miracle they needed.

Remember, the "Point of Contact" does not produce miracle power; rather, it is the pre-determined thing that causes you to release your faith. Faith produces miracles!

The account of Jairus and his little daughter is so full of dynamic truth that it would be a travesty of justice not to share some of the more salient facets with you.

Let's take a moment to review the story just as it is written in the Bible:

> *And, behold, there cometh one of the rulers of the synagogue, Jairus by name; and when he saw him, he fell at his feet, And besought him greatly, saying, My little daughter lieth at the point of death: I pray thee, come and lay thy hands on her, that she may be healed; and she shall live. And Jesus went with him...*

> MARK 5:22-24 KJV

The first lesson I want you to learn is the difference between fact and truth.

You may be saying, "Brother Cerullo, facts and truth are the same!"

Not so!

Let me explain!

When the father of the little girl fell down before Jesus he first of all spoke facts. He said "my little daughter lieth at the point of death."

That was a fact, but it was not the truth. If all the facts had been known the little girl was already past the point of death, she was dead!

Not that it made any difference because TRUTH, the very embodiment of resurrection LIFE, was on His way to her house.

Let me say it this way, "Facts cannot alter the truth, but truth can alter, change or re-arrange the facts as often as it chooses!"

Listen closely to the words of Jairus, "My little daughter lieth at the point of death." Those were the facts as he knew them, but he didn't stop there.

Now hear the rest of his words, because he didn't just speak facts, he also spoke truth. *"I pray thee, come and lay thy hands on her, that she may be healed; and she shall live."*

The man's faith must have been jumping up and down inside him when he spoke those powerful words of truth.

Jairus was saying to the Lord, I have established my "Point of Contact." It's all wrapped up in You laying Your hands on my little daughter. The moment Your hand touches her I will release my faith and she will be healed and SHE SHALL LIVE!

Every time I read this portion of Scripture I am blessed and encouraged by the reaction of Jesus to this man. The Lord didn't consult with His secretary to see if it would fit into His schedule for Him to go to Jairus' house. He simply went without hesitation!

Can you imagine, the Creator of the universe, the God of eternity, the very one who will rule over all the earth, was not too busy to go home with a man whose daughter lay dead?

As I have said many times, the measure of a preacher is not in his oratorical skills or his ability to sway an audience, but in the compassion he shows to the lost, the sick and the suffering.

A man cannot be measured by his ability to get the job done, but by the way he treats his fellow man. A leader is followed when he leads, not when he shouts orders.

Oftentimes, businessmen or preachers want to impress me by taking me to an expensive restaurant, but I'm impressed more by the way they treat the waitress than I am the place. If they are curt, demanding and tight-fisted with the server, I know they will be the same with me, if given the opportunity.

Respect cannot be demanded or bought, it must be earned!

The Lord was not too busy, nor was anything on His agenda more important than going to the home of Jairus to raise his daughter from the dead. And...He is not too busy to go to your house today, if you invite Him.

As they journeyed to Jairus' house they encountered a slight interruption. Do you recall the woman with the issue of blood from the previous chapter? This is where she fit into the picture. Jesus was on His way to Jairus' house when she pressed her way through the crowd and touched His garment.

I want you to get a mental picture of this scene, because it is so vital to your faith.

When the woman with the issue of blood touched the hem of Christ's garment, healing virtue flowed out of Him. That's when He stopped walking and asked, *"Who touched Me?"*

Obviously, when Jesus stopped the whole multitude also stopped, craned their necks to see what was happening and listened intently to the dialogue between the Lord and the woman.

Jairus had a front row view of all that was taking place. He heard the woman tell of her years of suffering and pain, all of which he could verify. Being the rabbi of the local synagogue Jairus certainly knew about the woman's condition and could in all probability call her by name.

It's one thing to read or hear about miracles in another city or country, but to witness one in someone you know is a great stimulus to anyone's faith.

I want you to see just how devious the devil can be.

Just as Jesus was capping off the tremendous miracle for the woman with the issue of blood by saying to her, *"Daughter, thy faith hath made thee whole; go in peace, and be whole of thy plague."*

Someone nudged Jairus and said,"...*Thy daughter is dead: why troublest thou the Master any further?*"

At the precise moment his faith would be sky-rocketing Jairus is given the most disconcerting news he had ever heard.

There is no way to put into words the shock a parent goes through when they hear the news that one of their children has died. The mind becomes numb, because the pain is so great. I speak from experience having lost a wonderful son.

I can empathize with Jairus, I know the sudden helplessness he felt as the stone cold words, *"your daughter is dead,"* hit his heart like a sledgehammer.

You could almost hear the menacing cackle of the demon of death as a pale of gloom started to creep across the face of Jairus, his only daughter was dead!

Indeed, *"...why trouble the Master any further?"*

This type of question flies in the face of God! Since when is it a trouble to Him to comfort the brokenhearted? Who said it was a bother to God to come to the aid of the hurting? Who is the originator of such a question and where is its birthplace?

I'll tell you where that comes from...the throne room of darkness and the wretched fiend who thought it up is Satan, the chief of devils! The very thought that it would *"trouble the Master,"* is an insult to the Son of God!

The question, *"...why trouble the Master any further?"* carried with it the implication that Christ was no match for death.

Death had reigned supreme through the centuries as man's most feared enemy.

The moment Cain murdered his brother, Able, death began its crusade on planet earth, making and keeping its appointment with every creature, whether fish, fowl, animal or human being...except...Enoch and Elijah!

31

This is not the time to elaborate on those two stalwarts of Old Testament fame, so let me simply say, through these two men, God proved to the world that even death is subject to His sovereign will and purpose.

Each time I read this story I'm impressed with the swiftness of the Lord in handling what could have been a fatal blow to the synagogue ruler's faith. He didn't give doubt, the "snake's" deadly venom, a chance to enter and defile Jairus' heart.

The Bible declares:

As soon as Jesus heard the word that was spoken, He saith unto the ruler of the synagogue, Be not afraid, only believe.
MARK 5:35-36KJV

With just five words, *"Be not afraid, only believe,"* Jesus counteracted the poison, defanged the snake and defeated the entire plot of the devil.

In essence the Lord said to Jairus, "You have established a powerful 'Point of Contact,' hold on to it, because nothing has changed!"

Head knowledge should never affect faith!

Let me reason with you!

If you believe God can heal a headache, what does it matter if a brain tumor is causing the pain? If you believe God can heal a stomachache, what does it matter if the pain is a result of an ulcer or cancer? A doctor's diagnosis should have no influence at all on your ability to trust God for your healing.

The Psalmist David said:

Praise the LORD, O my soul, and forget not all his benefits – who forgives all your sins and heals all your diseases,
PSALMS 103:2-3 NIV

Did you notice; the Word places no limits on the Lord's power to heal? It said, *"who forgives all your sins and heals all your diseases."*

The Word doesn't say, *"all... except... cancer, diabetes, high blood pressure, arthritis, kidney failure, ulcers, hypertension, rheumatism, blindness, heart trouble, deafness, or a myriad of other diseases."* Thank God it says, *He heals all your diseases!"*

When Jesus said to Jairus, *"Be not afraid, only believe,"* He put a torch to the devil's playhouse. Those five words must have reverberated through the corridors of hell. They spelled instant defeat for the hordes of darkness.

Any man who dares to arm himself with that powerful statement can stop the enemy dead in his tracks and the same is true for women and children. Simply put, the devil cannot stand up to anyone who is fearless and full of faith.

The challenge from the Lord, *"Be not afraid, only believe,"* struck the cord of courage in Jairus' heart because immediately they resumed their journey to his house.

LOUD WEEPING AND WAILING AWAITED THEM!

If you have never been to a Jewish mourning, you cannot imagine the frenzied fervor or the wild emotionalism that is often displayed.

When Jairus and the Lord arrived they were greeted with loud weeping and wailing. Some of the mourners may have felt genuine sorrow for the father and mother of the little girl, but others were there for the emotional high they received at such gatherings.

Why would I make such a statement? I'll show you!

As Jesus entered the house and saw the tumult, *"He said to them, 'Why make a commotion and weep? The child has not died, but is asleep.' And they began laughing at Him."* Mark 5:39 NAS

Let's talk about the mourner's reaction to Christ's words. If they were indeed sorrowful over the death of the child, wouldn't they have rejoiced that there was yet hope for her? Rather than rejoicing, they began to laugh and jeer at Him. That's hardly the response you expect from a person with a broken heart.

Did you notice how quickly the emotions changed? One minute they were weeping and wailing loudly and the next they were laughing at Him with contempt.

So, what did Christ do?

He put them all out of the house!

Here's something to think about, every person in the house could have witnessed one of the greatest miracles of all time but, they choose to doubt rather than believe.

Not one of them could have prevented the miracle from taking place; the devil had given it his best shot and failed, so I promise you none of them could keep it from happening! They simply laughed themselves out of God's divine presence.

What a loss it is when we allow doubt to cloud our minds so that we miss what God is saying and doing!

After putting out the unbelievers,

He took along the child's father and mother and His own companions, and entered the room where the child was.

MARK 5:40 NAS

Showdown Time

To Jairus it must have seemed as if the whole universe had come to a screeching halt. Everything that had happened from the moment he laid his eyes on the Master at the seashore, every word that had fallen from His lips was on the line...it was time for Him to produce a miracle or slip into oblivion. It was showdown time!

Either Christ was who He said He was, God's *"only begotten Son,"* or He was the worst imposter of all time and needed to be exposed for the charlatan He was.

Pardon me for shouting, but this needs to be proclaimed from the mountain tops for the world to hear...

THANK GOD! JESUS IS WHO HE CLAIMED TO BE! HE WAS AND IS AND WILL ALWAYS BE...EQUAL TO THE TEST!

Jairus didn't have to wait long to find out that Christ was more than a match for the devil, more than a match for any sickness and certainly more than a match for the angel of death.

Jesus was getting ready to prove to the father and the mother, to Peter, James, and John, that He was, at that moment, the "Resurrection and the Life!"   It was not something He would become at a later date.

After clearing the house of the doubters and scoffers, the Bible says: *"And taking the child by the hand,"* that was Jairus' cue, the moment for him to release his faith, remember he had established this as his "Point of Contact!"

Jairus had boldly proclaimed his faith back at the seashore, he believed the Master could heal his daughter's sickness when he said, *"come and lay thy hands on her, that she may be healed,"* but now it was worse than he had imagined, his little daughter was not sick, she was dead!

Could this itinerate Preacher from Nazareth reach through the mysterious veil, that stood as a silent guard between this world and the ethereal, and pull his loved one back to him? Would he once again have the joy of hearing her voice, seeing her smile and feeling her arms around his neck?

Or was it too late?

You will recall at the beginning of this chapter I explained the difference between facts and truth. This is a classic example. The fact is, the little girl was dead, but faith doesn't deal with facts, it deals with truth!

Regardless of what the situation looks like in the natural, when you establish a "Point of Contact", you are not bound by the facts, because you move in the realm of faith.

Standing on the shoreline of the Galilee, Jairus not only said, *"I pray thee, come and lay thy hands on her, that she may be healed;"* he also said, **"and she shall live."**

God loves to hear you make declarations of faith!

Before the messengers brought the debilitating news that his daughter was dead...before they reached his house and heard the sad wail of the mourners, faith had risen up big in the heart of Jairus and he had made the death defeating proclamation...

"she shall live!"

With hurt and pain all around you it's wonderful to read about an impossible situation with a happy ending, that's exactly what we have here.

When Jesus entered the room, He took the dead child's hand and He said to her, *"Talitha kum!:"* (which translated means, *"Little girl, I say to you, arise!"*).

It would be so easy to write how the words of Jesus brought the universe to a halt. That His voice rang down the corridors of hell and rattled the doors of the dungeon darkness or the world seemed to be in a state of suspended animation...but it didn't happen that way. The Bible declares:

And immediately the girl rose and began to walk...

MARK 5:39-43 NAS

In this chapter I have revealed two dynamic truths for your spiritual well being.

First, that you recognize the difference between facts and the truth. It's alright to state the facts of any given situation as long as you remember to speak the truth. In order for faith to respond to truth, it must not be bound up by facts

Facts view things as they appear to be, then confesses the impossible. Faith looks through the eyes of the Holy Spirit and announces loud and clear, *"With God all things are possible!"*

Second, it is crucial that you establish a "Point of Contact" as a release for your faith. And…having established your own "Point of Contact," don't succumb to temptation and become fearful or afraid when the enemy tries to overwhelm you as you journey toward your miracle.

The writer of Hebrews has a final word for you concerning your endurance when the tempter tries to sidetrack you:

> *Therefore, do not throw away your confidence, which has a great reward. For you have need of endurance, so that when you have done the will of God, you may receive what was promised.*

> HEBREWS 10:35-36 NAS

When you establish a "Point of Contact" don't expect the devil to run away and hide – after all – you are invading his territory and challenging his authority. Do it anyway…

The Reward is Magnificent!

Section One

Chapter 3
Look And Live

One would think the children of Israel were so happy to be out of bondage and away from the terrible taskmasters of Egypt, that they would have danced from the city limits of Goshen all the way to the Promised Land.

Except for Moses and the Egyptians who choose to be identified with the Israelis and join the exodus from the land of bondage, every person in the vast multitude was born and raised under the merciless whip of the Pharaoh's henchmen.

It's hard to imagine that these people had known nothing but slavery all their life, their father's life, their grandfather's life, their great, and their great-great for four hundred years. If you put all the "great-greats" together it would look like the "Wongs" in a Chinese telephone directory.

Sadly, slavery was not simply a physical malady with those people...they had a slave-mentality as well.

The words "slave-mentality," have little meaning to the people of the free world, so let me give you a classic example that will open your understanding to the true definition.

When the Holy Spirit ripped the moorings from beneath the Iron Curtain and it came crashing down, millions of people in what was known as the Soviet Union became angered.

Angered because they could no longer rely on the government to feed, clothe and provide a place for them to live. Very few, if any of them remembered life prior to the Bolshevik Revolution, so all they knew was to live, dependent on the benevolence of the state.

Hard work, pride of ownership, savings accounts and individual accomplishment were not in their vocabulary.

They quickly forgot the long bread lines, the sub-par living quarters, and shoddy workmanship of products produced by workers who took no pride in what they made, because there were no incentives to do or be better.

The Soviets were a 20th Century repeat of ancient Israel in that they had a slave-mentality! Freedom to them was paramount to someone killing the goose that laid the golden egg.

I love liberty so much that I cannot imagine anyone choosing bondage over freedom, death over life or poverty over abundance!

Yet...there are multiplied millions throughout the length and breadth of the earth who prefer not to think for themselves. I read once that the experts say, only 5% of the people think, 10% think they think and 85% think it's work to think.

Most folks find it easier to follow the crowd than to draw a line in the sand and stand as a person of dignity, creativity and independence.

Having witnessed one of the most awesome miracles of all

time, the parting of the Red Sea, and having been given a guided tour through the world's largest aquarium, the children of Israel should have set a straight course, with shofars and tambourines in hand, to the land flowing with milk and honey.

But they didn't!

Instead, they began a forty year traipse through the barren wastelands. Their actions proved that had they been allowed to enter the Promised Land with their debilitated, slave-mentality, they would have quietly capitulated to the giants and become servants to the ungodly in the very land they were to possess.

By the fortieth year in the desert it seems as if the people would have outgrown their childish ways, but some bad habits are passed on from generation to generation. Grumbling and complaining are two examples of generational hand-me-downs!

After all the wonderful miracles they had seen and the battles they had won, the children of Israel should have been ready to march in and conqueror the Promised Land, but rebellion reared its ugly head and they started murmuring again.

The Word says:

And the people spoke against God and Moses, Why have you brought us up out of Egypt to die in the wilderness? For there is no food and no water, and we loathe this miserable food.
NUMBERS 21:5 NAS

When you read this verse it sounds as if they had just left Egypt, the truth is, they had been in the desert forty years!

In that crowd, anyone younger than thirty-nine years old

had never seen Pharaoh or the pyramids, never tasted the leeks and garlic or eaten from the fabled flesh pots of Egypt. But...they allowed the same grumbling, complaining spirit their parents brought with them from the land of bondage to control them.

They didn't realize how good they had it. Gone and forgotten were the taskmasters making them build cities, no whips lashed their backs when they didn't make enough bricks and their babies were not sacrificed to the Egyptian Nile River gods.

Look at their complaint again, *there is no food and no water.* No food and no water? They had been in the wilderness for forty years witnessing the greatest miracles of supply the world has ever recorded.

Let me give you just two statistics that will blow your imagination and to think the Lord did this for them for forty years without missing a single day:

- He provided over 9 million meals every day! That was just for the people; we have no idea how many sheep, goats, cows, donkeys and camels He also provided food for.
- He supplied more than 4 million gallons, clean drinking water daily. Add to that massive volume enough water for them to bathe and to launder their clothes, plus enough for all the animals to drink.

God did all of this in the desert without the aid of men or governments. Not one morning throughout the entire forty years did He wake Moses up and tell him that he was running short that day and the people would have to fend for themselves.

Every day except Saturday, the Sabbath, at sun-up, the

manna was on the ground ready to be gathered. For the Sabbath, God gave a double portion on Friday morning.

Regardless of what God did for them they were not thankful in their heart to Him.

Notice what the Psalmist said:

They even spoke against God himself. *"Why can't he give us decent food as well as water?"* they grumbled.

Jehovah heard them and was angry; the fire of his wrath burned against Israel because they didn't believe in God or trust in him to care for them, even though he commanded the skies to open -- he opened the windows of heaven -- and rained down manna for their food. He gave them bread from heaven! They ate angels' food! He gave them all they could hold.

PSALMS 78:19-25 TLB

Did you notice the Psalmist described the manna as "angels' food?"

To top off all the insults the people threw this slur in the face of God, *"we loathe this miserable food."* How could anyone "loathe" manna? You could boil, fry, broil, bake, stew, fricassee or eat it just as it came from heaven. It was always fresh and always delicious.

That statement "we loathe this miserable food" was the last straw! Immediately, God withdrew His divine hand of protection from about them:

And the LORD sent fiery serpents among the people and they bit the people; so that many people of Israel died. So the people came to Moses and said, We have sinned, because we have spoken against the LORD and you; intercede with the LORD, that He may remove the serpents from us. And Moses interceded for the people. Then the LORD said to Moses, 'Make a fiery serpent, and

43

set it on a standard; and it shall come about, that everyone who is bitten, when he looks at it, he shall live.

NUMBERS 21:6-8 NAS

I want you to see an important truth that is tucked away in this portion of the story. God does not always answer our prayers exactly as we pray them, but His answers are far better than what we ask.

Here is an example!

The people were begging Moses to ask God to remove the serpents. While that would have been a wonderful miracle, it would have done nothing for those who had already been bitten.

God had a better idea!

He gave them a "Powerful Point of Contact" that rebuked death and made the serpent's bite ineffective. Wow! One more time God was showing the Israelites and the world that He is the mighty God and nothing is impossible with Him.

The serpents slithered through the congregation coiling and striking with reckless abandon. Men, women and children were the hapless victims of these fiery messengers whose only mission was to spread their deadly venom and kill!

In wide-eyed horror mothers watched the poison creep up the legs of their children knowing that when it reached the heart, that life-giving vessel would recoil from the venomous invasion and stop pumping. Death would seize its prey, life would be over!

Husbands watched in dazed disbelief as their wife's forehead dripped with perspiration while the deadly poison from the serpent's bite won the battle against life.

Wives looked on in forlorn helplessness as their strong, healthy husband convulsed from the nauseating effect of the snake's toxin attacking his nervous system.

This Bible account reminds me of a story I read about a young Indian scout who was going through the initiation rites for becoming a brave.

One of the things he was required to do was to climb to the top of a mountain and bring an eagle feather back to the chief.

When he reached the top of the mountain he found not one, but two beautiful eagle feathers among the craggy rocks.

As he reached for one of the feathers he suddenly withdrew his hand because a rattlesnake was coiled near the feather. The young Indian moved cautiously, so as not to disturb what he thought was a sleeping killer.

To his amazement the snake spoke to him saying, "please, take me to the valley, I'm dying from the cold."

"No!" The young man protested, "if I take you down you'll bite me and I will die!"

"The cold is killing me," the snake replied, "if you will take me down to the valley, I promise I won't bite you."

So the young Indian picked up the snake, put it in his pouch and started down the mountain. As he descended the temperature changed and the snake began to revive.

When he approached the valley floor he reached into the pouch to remove the snake, as he did, the serpent bit him.

The young man cried, "You promised you wouldn't bite me if I brought you down and saved your life!"

The rattler replied, "You knew I was a snake when you picked me up."

You can trust a snake to always be a snake and you can trust the devil to always be the devil. Just as you can never turn a rattlesnake into a house-pet, you can't make a saint out of a devil.

We must always be on guard, because the slimy serpent from the pit of darkness will lie, deceive and poison anyone he possibly can.

The very people that God called His own, those whom He rescued from tyranny, broke the bands of slavery and brought out of bondage; had once again allowed sin to derail their journey to the Promised Land.

As a result, sin threw open the door for the destroyer to come in among them, flash his deadly fangs and spew his poison over their hallowed camp.

As bad as the rebellion was, God did not, could not, forsake His own. Perhaps it was in recalling this tragic encounter and the Lord's marvelous grace that inspired King David to write:

> *Just as a father has compassion on his children, So the LORD has compassion on those who fear Him. For He Himself knows our frame; He is mindful that we are but dust.*
>
> PSALMS 103:13-14 NAS

God, however, was not finished! Even though His people had sinned grievously, because of His infinite love and mercy, He gave them the formula for victory. *"...the LORD said to Moses, 'Make a fiery serpent, and set it on a standard; and it shall come about, that everyone who is bitten, when he looks at it, he will live'"* (Numbers 21:8 NAS).

God established a "Powerful Point of Contact" for the entire nation. Notice what He said: *"and it shall come about, that everyone who is bitten, when he looks at it, he will live."*

Knowing human nature as I do, I'm certain that some of the people refused to even look, because they did not believe that something so simple as looking at the brazen serpent could negate the deadly effects of the snakes venom.

Unbelief is terrible...it corrupts the mind! It hinders men and women from making spiritual progress and ultimately causes them to accept less than God's best for their life.

Do you remember the statement I made earlier, that God doesn't always give you exactly what you ask for, He oftentimes gives you much, much more? This is a perfect example of God doing far more than they requested.

They asked God to get rid of the serpents, instead, God gave them an antidote for the poison and in so doing, He gave them life for death.

And Moses made a bronze serpent and set it on the standard; and it came about, that if a serpent bit any man, when he looked to the bronze serpent, he lived.

NUMBERS 21:9 NAS

I want you to grasp the importance of the "Powerful Point of Contact" God provided for them.

Unlike the points of contact we discussed earlier, such as, the woman touching the hem of Christ's garment. Or Jairus declaring that his "Point of Contact" to release his faith for a miracle was the moment Jesus laid His hands on his dying child. The brazen serpent was God's divine "Point of Contact."

I must emphasize again the purpose for a "Point of Contact," lest some make the same tragic mistake the children of Israel made with the brazen serpent.

It is a specific moment in time or a unique place or a particular act that you have established in your heart to release your faith and believe God for your answer.

It was not Christ's garment that healed the woman of the issue of blood, it was her faith that produced the miracle. In the same manner, when Jairus heard that his daughter was dead, the Lord's admonition to him was, "Be not afraid, only believe." In essence Jesus was saying to the man, your faith is the catalyst that will create the miracle you are seeking.

The brazen serpent was not the healer!

We must be certain that we never, *Never, NEVER*, worship a *"Point of Contact"!*

Let me explain!

The children of Israel were so blessed by the miracle of the brazen serpent that they carried it with them the rest of the way through the wilderness and into the Promised Land.

At some point in time, however, the truth of their marvelous deliverance became distorted. Rather than seeing the brazen serpent as a testimony of God's glorious, healing power, they gave the snake a name, "Nehushtan," and began to worship it as though it had healing power.

The brazen serpent was not the healer, nor is any other object. These were and are "Powerful Points of Contact," nothing more!

In our crusades, seminars and conferences when the anointing of the Holy Spirit comes upon me, I feel the power of God coursing through my body until my hands are literally on fire.

As a result of this powerful anointing, multiplied thousands of men and women have been healed and delivered when I lay my hands upon them.

Knowing that God has anointed my hands with His holy fire, many people use that as their "Powerful Point of Contact!" They believe the moment I touch them they will receive a miracle from God, and they do!

We have documented evidence in our files of not hundreds, but thousands of miracles the Lord has performed when I laid hands on the blind, deaf, lame, crippled, AIDS victims, those with cancer, tumors, diabetes, ulcers, arthritis, rheumatism, emphysema, asthma, heart trouble, goiters, mental conditions and every other known malady.

But…it is not me and it's not my hands that heal or perform miracles. **Jesus Christ, the Son of the living God is the Healer!** My hands are the "Powerful Point of Contact" that multiplied thousands use to release their faith for a miracle.

They believe the moment I touch them they will be healed. It is Christ's power and their faith that sets them free, my hands are simply their "Point of Contact."

Oh, that the children of Israel could have realized that the brazen serpent was simply a God given "Point of Contact" for them to release their faith and receive a miracle, it was not an object of worship.

They took their unique "Point of Contact", which was so powerful that all they had to do was look at it and life prevailed over death, and turned it into idolatry.

In the New Testament Paul spoke of it in this manner:

Because when they knew and recognized Him as God, they did not honor and glorify Him as God or give Him thanks. But instead they became futile and godless in their thinking [with vain imaginings, foolish reasoning, and stupid speculations] and their senseless minds were darkened. Claiming to be wise, they became fools [professing to be smart, they made simpletons of themselves]. And by them the glory and majesty and excellence of the immortal God were exchanged for and represented by images, resembling mortal man and birds and beasts and reptiles. Therefore God gave them up in the lusts of their [own] hearts, to sexual impurity, to the dishonoring of their bodies among themselves [abandoning them to the degrading power of sin], Because they exchanged the truth of God for a lie and worshiped and served the creature rather than the Creator, Who is blessed for ever. Amen.

ROMANS 1:21-25

AMP

Imagine, one of the greatest mass miracles in the Old Testament was effectuated by God giving His people a "Powerful Point of Contact." All they had to do was **Look and Live.**

You no longer look at a brazen serpent as your "Point of Contact" for receiving a miracle. Rather, you look to God to inspire you with an individual Rhema or a fresh anointed Word from the Lord.

Or...you may adopt the same "Powerful Point of Contact" that has proven successful to multiplied thousands throughout the world. You can set your heart to believe that the moment my hand touches you, your miracle will be granted.

The author of the Book of Hebrews said it so succinctly:

Therefore, do not throw away your confidence, which has a great reward. For you have need of endurance, so that when you have done the will of God, you may receive what was promised.

HEBREWS 10:35-36 NAS

A miracle, a wonderful, glorious miracle or some other dynamic answer to prayer is awaiting you! All you need to do is establish a "Powerful Point of Contact," release your faith and watch God do the rest.

Remember...your "Powerful Point of Contact" is exactly that, a "Point of Contact" to release your faith and receive a miracle. Whether it is my hands or another person's hands, a prayer shawl or a special place you have been directed by the Holy Spirit to go to, you are never to worship the "Point of Contact!" Worship God!

It is your faith that releases the power of God in your life, not the "Point of Contact."

Your faith knows that God is bigger than any sickness, disease, heartache, problem or dilemma you may be facing. Your "Powerful Point of Contact" releases your faith and allows your Great, Big, Wonderful God to work for you!

Section One

Chapter 4

Speak The Word And My Servant Will Be Healed!

Faith can get more from God in a moment of time than a lifetime of begging, because faith has the enviable ability to tug at the Lord's heartstrings and get answers when everything else seems to fail.

I've known people, as I'm sure you have also, who make begging and pleading with God a full time job.

Jesus outlined the three things we are to employ in our approach to God:

- Ask

- Seek

- Knock

When He said, *"Ask,"* He did not mean beg or plead. With God it is not the length...but the strength of your prayer.

This is not to say that it's not necessary to spend sufficient time in prayer. The Bible speaks of Jesus praying all night:

And it was at this time that He went off to the mountain to pray, and He spent the whole night in prayer to God.

LUKE 6:12 NAS

53

And after He had sent the crowds away, He went up to the mountain by Himself to pray; and when it was evening, He was there alone. And in the fourth watch of the night (between three and six in the morning) He came to them, walking on the sea.

MATTHEW 14:23; 25 NAS

We know that on the night of His arrest Jesus had been praying for at least three hours before Judas betrayed Him with a kiss, and the high priest with his band of lying thugs arrested Him (Matthew 26:40-44; Mark 14:37-41).

Paul the Apostle knew the value of intercessory prayer, for he said to the church in Thessalonica;

[And we] continue to pray especially and with most intense earnestness night and day that we may see you face to face and mend and make good whatever may be imperfect and lacking in your faith.

I THESSALONIANS 3:10 AMP

He also interceded for Timothy as he said: *"...I constantly remember you in my prayers night and day."* II Timothy 1:3 NAS

And in his instructions to Timothy, Paul admonished:

Now [a woman] who is a real widow and is left entirely alone and desolate has fixed her hope on God and perseveres in supplications and prayers night and day.

I TIMOTHY 5:5 AMP

Again, there is nothing wrong with praying long prayers as long as they are not religious mumbo-jumbo or empty repetitions.

Jesus warned:

Don't recite the same prayer over and over as the heathen do, who think prayers are answered only by repeating them again and again...

MATTHEW 6:7 TLB

Let me give you a wonderful example of true intercessory prayer and of establishing a "Powerful Point of Contact!"

And when He (Jesus) had entered Capernaum, a centurion came to Him, imploring Him, and saying, Lord, my servant is lying paralyzed at home, fearfully tormented. Jesus said to him, I will come and heal him. But the centurion said, Lord, I am not worthy for You to come under my roof, but just say the word, and my servant will be healed. For I, also, am a man under authority, with soldiers under me; and I say to this one, Go! and he goes, and to another, Come! and he comes, and to my slave, Do this! and he does it. Now when Jesus heard this, He marveled, and said to those who were following, Truly I say to you, I have not found such faith with anyone in Israel.

MATTHEW 8:5-10 NAS

What was it about this man that he could exhibit such great faith that it caused the Lord to single him out and comment to the multitude that He had not found his equal in Israel?

First, he understood authority!

The centurion knew that everyone beneath him militarily had to obey his orders or face the consequences. When he spoke he had the backing of legions of Roman soldiers and if need be, even Caesar. Because of his authority the centurion had a certain degree of invincibility.

The centurion's words carried blessings or curses, freedom or incarceration, life or death...but...when he spoke to Jesus he subjected himself totally to Christ's authority.

Look at the first word out of the centurion's mouth. *"Lord!"* By addressing Jesus as Lord, he actually elevated Him above Caesar, which was considered treason against the crown.

Christ's attention was immediately captured by this man who in essence laid his life on the line by calling Him Lord.

With that simple act the centurion placed Jesus on the throne of his heart and denounced every other god for the Word says:

> *...no one can say that Jesus is Lord except by the Holy Spirit.*
>
> I CORINTHIANS 12:3 NKJ

Can you imagine how many prayers would get answered if every child of God approached His throne affirming Him as Lord above all others?

Notice the simplicity of the man's intercession, *"my servant is lying paralyzed at home, fearfully tormented."* His prayer was not a long drawn out affair. He didn't try to convince the Lord of his or the servant's worthiness of a miracle.

Rather, the prayer was straight forward and to the point... *"my servant is lying paralyzed at home, fearfully tormented."*

Through the years I have watched and listened to men and women all over the world pray, I have seen tears of anguish and tears of joy as hearts were opened up to the Lord.

I've also observed those who think they will impress God with a tearful voice, but no real tears.

It makes me want to tell them, if you are going to cry before the Lord, be sure you have tears in your eyes as well as your voice, otherwise you are just whining and neither God nor men enjoy listening to anyone whine.

As I said earlier, it was not the length of the centurion's prayer, but the strength of his positive, faith-filled intercession that brought an immediate response from the Lord.

"I will come and heal him."

No sooner had Jesus offered to go to his home than the centurion replied: *"Lord, I am not worthy for You to come under my roof."*

The man was not living under the false illusion that he deserved a miracle. He recognized and confessed his own unworthiness...but he didn't stop there, his faith carried him to the next level with God where miracles are created.

We can learn a great deal by observing the way he uses the conjunctive word "but." *"But just say the word, and my servant will be healed.*

With this statement we get our first glimpse of the centurion's "Powerful Point of Contact." It was Christ's authority to command the spirit of sickness to leave his servant!

When he said to Jesus, *"say the word,"* he was acknowledging the divine power and authority over all the power of the devil that was resident in Christ.

In effect he was saying, "You are the Commander in Chief of a force mightier and more powerful than the vaunted, world conquering, Roman Army."

The centurion recognized that his authority was limited to ordering men to come and go, but Christ's authority was unlimited!

Men could and did disobey his commands, even when it meant death or imprisonment, but Christ's authority left no room for disobedience, for He controlled the universe.

Sickness, disease, death, heartache, pain and suffering were all in the scope of Christ's authority. But it didn't stop there…with one breath He controlled the wind and the waves.

He could break a single loaf of bread and feed thousands, yet still have enough left over to fill several baskets. He could look at a pot full of water and change it to the finest wine.

Demons by the legions were no match for the Master

On the shore of the beautiful Sea of Galilee Jesus drove a legion of devils out of a man with the one small word, "go." Then He sent the once, wild man from the tombs to the towns with the glorious Good News.

Earlier I asked the question, "What was it about the centurion that he could exhibit such great faith it caused the Lord to single him out and comment to the multitude that He had not found his equal in Israel?

First, he understood authority!

In his heart the centurion never questioned the authority of Christ. As a commander of men, his words were backed by Caesar. When he spoke men trembled with fear. A simple word from his lips could mean life or sudden death. But his authority was nothing compared to that of Jesus Christ and he knew it!

Second, he had tremendous perception!

He perceived that Jesus Christ was the Commander in Chief of the Spirit world and the only thing necessary for Him to do was speak to the demon of sickness that had his servant bound.

Let this truth sink deep into your spirit. When Jesus offered to go to the centurion's house he told the Lord, You don't need to take one step in that direction.

In truth he was saying, Lord there is no such thing as distance with You. Standing right where You are, Your voice will reverberate throughout the universe, every angel in heaven will snap to attention and every demon, including Satan himself will tremble and shake in fear. **Simply speak the word!**

No wonder Jesus responded with such a strong approval, the centurion actually saw Him for Who He is. The man was not seeing Christ through the eyes of a natural man or even those of a Roman Soldier, he saw Him through the eyes of faith.

By seeing and acknowledging Christ for Who He is, the centurion was able to establish a "Powerful Point of Contact" through which to release his faith.

This story is so different from that of Naaman in the Old Testament.

Let me paraphrase the story for you!

Naaman was greatly admired by the king of Syria for his heroism. He was the highest ranking officer in the Syrian Army and he was a mighty man of valor. But...he was a leper!

During one of his raids on an Israeli village, a young Jewish girl was taken captive and became a servant to Naaman's wife.

The story at this point takes a beautiful twist.

Loneliness for home and family and bitterness over having been taken captive and forced into a life of slavery could have filled the young Israeli girl's heart.

She no doubt saw the leprous spots spreading on Naaman's hand and arm and heard the hopeless, hushed whispers between the great soldier and his wife.

She could have said in her heart, "Let him die with that terrible disease eating away his flesh! He has it coming, he's inflicted so much pain and suffering in other people's lives, it's good enough for him!"

But...she didn't!

Rather than becoming bitter and vindictive over her sad misfortune she became a missionary for the Lord.

The young lady said to Naaman's wife:

...I wish that my master were with the prophet who is in Samaria! Then he would cure him of his leprosy.

II KINGS 5:3 NAS

As soon as the king of Syria heard that there was a cure in Israel for the dreaded disease he dispatched Naaman with a letter to the king of Israel.

He also included a large sum of money to pay for the expected treatment: ...So Naaman started out, taking gifts of $20,000 in silver, $60,000 in gold, and ten suits of clothing.

II KINGS 5:5 TLB

This is not the time or place to go into the evident, illogical thinking of the king of Syria and Naaman, for rather than going to the Prophet Elisha, he went to the king of Israel.

I can tell you this; it caused quite a stir when Naaman arrived at the palace in Samaria with the letter telling the king that he was expected to heal the man of his leprosy.

The prophet sent word to the king, don't tear your robe, send him to me and he will know there is a prophet in Israel.

When Naaman arrived at the prophet's home, Elisha didn't so much as go outside to meet him, he simply sent his servant with this message:

Go and wash in the Jordan seven times, and your flesh shall be restored to you and you shall be clean.

II KINGS 5:10 NAS

I want you to pause for a moment and gather your

thoughts, because my next statement should trigger something inside you that will help you know how to discern between your own thinking and a "Powerful Point of Contact".

Naaman became furious when the prophet's words, *"Go and wash in the Jordan seven times,"* he said, *"Behold, I thought, 'He will surely come out to me, and stand and call on the name of the LORD his God, and wave his hand over the place, and cure the leper."*

Here is the important thing I want you to see and recognize; the Prophet Elisha gave Naaman his "Powerful Point of Contact" when he said, *"Go and wash in the Jordan seven times,"* but Naaman had preconceived thoughts.

Notice his thoughts were not inspired of God or directed by the Holy Spirit, just a preconceived notion.

There is nothing wrong with having your own thoughts, but don't be so head-strong that when the prophet of God gives you inspired instructions you get furious. Naaman was looking for a religious ceremony while Elisha was presenting a "Powerful Point of Contact" that would result in a miracle.

It was not until his servants came to him and said,

> *My father, had the prophet told you to do some great thing, would you not have done it? How much more then, when he says to you, 'Wash, and be clean?*

II Kings 5:13 NAS

Naaman's "Powerful Point of Contact" was not in having the prophet pray and wave his hand over the leprosy but... *"Wash, and be clean."* When he did what the man of God told him to do, the leprosy vanished and his flesh was as fresh as a child's.

In the stories of these two men, each one was a great soldier in his own right, but they were terribly diverse in their approach to God.

Naaman, in the Old Testament, came to the man of God prepared to buy his cure. He was encumbered with ideas as to how the ceremony had to take place and became furious when the prophet didn't perform to his preconceived religious standard.

The New Testament soldier on the other hand humbly approached Christ full of faith and expectation. Absent of religiosity, he had established a "Powerful Point of Contact" upon which he could release his faith and receive a miracle answer for his servant.

"Just say the word, and my servant will be healed." The Roman Centurion said to the Commander of the universe, *"Say the word,"* and his sickness will have to flee. *"Say the word,"* and the demon's power will be broken…simply ***"say the word!"***

> *And Jesus said to the centurion, 'Go your way; let it be done to you as you have believed.'*

End of story? Not quite, you see anyone could have uttered those words, the proof of Christ's glorious power was what the centurion found when he arrived at his home.

The Word doesn't give us the details of the happy reunion; instead we are left to our own imaginations.

Here's what I think took place.

Just as the centurion reached for the handle the door opened and he saw the smiling face of his beloved servant who quickly bowed before him.

I can almost hear the centurion say, "stand up, let me look at you. When I left you were in bed, paralyzed and in great pain. How do you feel? Move your arms, now your hands, move your legs, bend over, now straighten up. Where is your pain?"

"Master," the servant answered, "I was in such pain I

thought I was going to die, but worse than the pain was the helpless feeling I had. I couldn't move my arms or my legs; I could only imagine myself lying there in that helpless condition until death finally seized my body.

But...a few minutes ago a holy presence came into my room more powerful than the sickness that had bound me. Suddenly, without explanation, the terrible pain was gone and I felt life throughout my body, the paralysis was gone and I was healed!"

You can draw your own conclusion as to how it happened since the Word simply declares:

"And the servant was healed that very hour."

The centurion had established a "Powerful Point of Contact" for his faith. It was not based on religious philosophy or man-made ideas, but on the concrete belief that Jesus Christ is God in the flesh and that nothing is too hard for Him.

Being a man with limited authority he respected the unlimited authority of Christ over all the power of the devil. He knew in his heart that a single word from the Lord was sufficient to heal his servant.

When Jesus said, *"Go your way; let it be done to you as you have believed,"* the centurion's faith was released, because that was his "Powerful Point of Contact!"

Remember, a preconceived religious notion is not the same as a "Powerful Point of Contact." Remember Naaman! He almost walked away from his miracle, because it did not come packaged in the religious garb he expected.

Be sensitive to the Holy Spirit...

Your miracle is only a word...

A touch...a confession away!

Section One

Chapter 5
The Devil Couldn't Stay

On more than one occasion Jesus dealt directly with gentiles. Each time there was something remarkable in their faith that set them apart from the crowd. The Roman Centurion in the previous chapter was a great example, he was a gentile, yet his faith was stronger than any displayed among the children of Israel.

Those to whom God had revealed His secrets and given the Law, the people He chose as His own, were bound up in religious tradition. Rather than walking by faith they measured the steps they could take on the Sabbath Day.

The Israelites were careful to wash their hands when they came from the market, because they dared not eat with unclean hands, but they were unconcerned about the avarice, the pride or the sin in their hearts.

Sadly, the Jews of Christ's time placed all their stock in who they were not to, Whom they belonged. Faith was a forgotten ingredient in their religion as the rabbis argued daily over the "jots and tittles" of the Law.

It is easy to understand why Jesus was moved by the sheer acts of faith from the gentiles, as in the instance of the Syrophenician woman who requested a miracle of deliverance for her daughter.

We pick up her story from Matthew's Gospel:

...behold, a woman who was a Canaanite from that district came out and, with [a loud, troublesomely urgent] cry, begged, Have mercy on me, O Lord, Son of David! My daughter is miserably and distressingly and cruelly possessed by a demon! But He did not answer her a word. And His disciples came and implored Him, saying, Send her away, for she is crying out after us. He answered, I was sent only to the lost sheep of the house of Israel. But she came and, kneeling, worshiped Him and kept praying, Lord, help me! And He answered, It is not right (proper, becoming, or fair) to take the children's bread and throw it to the little dogs. She said, Yes, Lord, yet even the little pups (little whelps) eat the crumbs that fall from their [young] masters' table. Then Jesus answered her, O woman, great is your faith! Be it done for you as you wish. And her daughter was cured from that moment.

MATTHEW 15:22-28 AMP

Right from the start the woman had to fight an uphill battle. She was rebuffed by the disciples and on the surface it looked as if she was denigrated by the Lord Himself.

Her approach was quite unique for a gentile, from three aspects, she cried, *"Have mercy on me, O Lord, Son of David!"*

Here's why I say her prayer was so unique:

First, she asked for mercy. The thing that makes this so extraordinary is that every false religion is based on appeasing an angry god.

In paganism, mercy is unheard of! The meaning of the word, "not getting what I deserve," was just as foreign to the idolatrous teaching of her day as it is today.

Secular humanism is a prime example of what idolatry is

all about. The "humanists" of today know nothing about mercy, their philosophy is that you are your own god and whatever happens to you is of your own making.

I shudder when I think of what it would be like to live my life and face God in eternity without His divine mercy. My heart joins with the Psalmist David in saying:

I will sing of the mercies of the LORD forever; with my mouth will I make known Your faithfulness to all generations.

PSALMS 89:1 NKJ

Second, she called Him "Lord!"

I find this particularly interesting since the Word declares, *"...no one can say that Jesus is Lord except by the Holy Spirit."*

I Corinthians 12:3 NKJ

Without question the Holy Spirit was working in the Syrophenician woman's heart, prompting her to confess Jesus as the Lord of her life. Isn't this exactly what Paul taught us to do in his letter to the Romans?

That if thou shalt confess with thy mouth the Lord Jesus, and shalt believe in thine heart that God hath raised him from the dead, thou shalt be saved. For with the heart man believeth unto righteousness; and with the mouth confession is made unto salvation. For the scripture saith, Whosoever believeth on him shall not be ashamed. For there is no difference between the Jew and the Greek: for the same Lord over all is rich unto all that call upon him. For whosoever shall call upon the name of the Lord shall be saved.

ROMANS 10:9-13 KJV

To confess Him as Lord, she had to tear herself away from idols her people worshiped as gods, including Allah, and his female counterpart Alat.

Yes, this is the same Allah that millions worship as god today. This demon-god of hatred, spiritual imprisonment and wanton murder; the one that humiliates women and degrades anyone who dares to speak against his ruthlessness, was only one of the many gods of ancient Canaan.

When the woman of Canaan confessed Christ as Lord, she divested herself of any and all allegiance to Allah, Alat and any other pagan deity.

Third, the woman called Him the "Son of David!"

How did this woman, a gentile, know to call Him the "Son of David?" How did she recognize Him as the rightful heir to that illustrious throne? What could that title possibly mean to her?

Her family, her race, her ancestors had, no doubt, been displaced, conquered, subjugated and subdued by the Israeli army when they possessed the land hundreds of years before.

So how did she quell the tumultuous storm of protest that raged in the hearts of any remaining Canaanites against the Jews?

She recognized Jesus as the Messiah, the promised Redeemer of all mankind.

Take note of this very important truth, when she cried out, *"Have mercy on me, O Lord, Son of David,"* she was literally confessing Him as the supreme Commander of the Heavenly Host and the rightful Heir to the eternal throne of King David!

The Syrophenician woman had great faith and her "Powerful Point of Contact" to release that faith was perseverance.

As I stated earlier in this chapter, she had an uphill battle from the very beginning. First, she was ignored by the Lord when she attempted to get a miracle for her child. She cried, *"My daughter is miserably and distressingly and cruelly possessed by a demon!" But... "He did not answer her a word."*

Was Jesus being cruel or unkind to this woman? No! He knew He was going to grant her a miracle, His motive was to get the attention of His followers, so they would learn the importance of perseverance.

Notice the dialogue between the Lord and His chosen men!

His disciples came and implored Him, saying, Send her away, for she is crying out after us. He answered, I was sent only to the lost sheep of the house of Israel.

Send her away? Where would she go, back to the lifeless pagan gods of the Canaanites? Could she turn to the Jewish Rabbis? They were the ordained keepers of the law, but they lacked the power or desire to free her daughter from the clutches of an evil spirit.

For Christ to send her away would be worse than a hospital refusing to care for the sick. Worse than a doctor refusing to treat a patient or a judge condemning an innocent man to die.

Would this Man of love and compassion, this One who was so generous and kind turn a deaf ear to a seeking heart? Could He, the Giver of life, be persuaded by His followers to abandon a seeking soul?

Were the chosen twelve so naive that they really thought He would send her away without fulfilling her desire?

While Jesus was sent only to the lost sheep of the house of Israel, that didn't preclude Him from accepting the gentiles who came to Him for salvation, healing and deliverance. The Syrophenician woman came to the right Person for a miracle.

In the midst of the conversation between Jesus and His disciples the Bible says:

But she came and, kneeling, worshiped Him and kept praying, Lord, help me!

If I can indelibly stamp in your memory the next four things the woman did and convince you to do them, you'll be light years ahead of the majority of people when it comes to getting your miracle from God.

1. She came to Jesus and the Word has promised that if you:

Come to Me, all who are weary and heavy-laden, and I will give you rest.
MATTHEW 11:28 NAS

Come near to God...he will come near to you.
JAMES 4:8 NIV

When she came near to Christ, the eternal, the everlasting Word obligated Him to draw near to her. The same is true for you! The very underpinning, the foundation of the Word is God's faithfulness. Settle it once-and-for-all in your heart that drawing near to God is always rewarded by Him drawing near to you.

2. She knelt before Him. I can't simply pass over this important gesture. In kneeling before the Master she confessed Him to be the King of her life. Through this act she paid Him the highest form of praise.

According to the Word: kneeling before Him is something that everyone will do some day:

...that to me every knee will bow, every tongue will swear allegiance.
Isaiah 45:23 NAS

This prophecy was reconfirmed in the New Testament:

For it is written, 'As I live, says the Lord, every knee shall bow to Me, and every tongue shall give praise to God.'
ROMANS 14:11 NAS

that at the name of Jesus every knee shall bow in heaven and on earth and under the earth, and every tongue shall confess that Jesus Christ is Lord, to the glory of God the Father.

PHILIPPIANS 2:10-11 TLB

Make no mistake, every man, woman, boy and girl will eventually bow before the Lord Jesus and confess that He is Lord. Sadly, some will do it on Judgment Day, when it is eternally too late.

The Canaanite bowed her knee to honor the Son of God!

3. She worshiped Him!

Worship is one of the most important and rewarding spiritual activities an individual ever engages in. It's important, because God seeks out those who worship Him. Observe what Jesus said to the woman of Samaria:

...an hour is coming, and now is, when the true worshippers will worship the Father in spirit and truth; for such people the Father seeks to be His worshippers.

JOHN 4:23 NAS

God hasn't changed; He is still seeking those who worship, (humbly adore) Him! To worship means that you want Him, His will, His purpose, His plan to be accomplished in your life and that loving Him is the uppermost thought in your mind.

Think of it this way, if you are a true worshippers of God, whenever you are seeking after and searching for Him, at that same time He is seeking you out to bless and fulfill your hearts desire.

The Syrophenician woman worshiped Christ. She humbled herself and fell at His feet in total submission.

4. And she kept praying!

Not enough can be said about the subject of prayer! This

is the avenue through which we communicate with God. Prayer is like breathing, exhaling and inhaling. When you exhale you are talking to God; when you inhale you are listening, while God talks to you.

Most folks never get to the latter part. They treat their prayer time like the Old MacDonald nursery rhyme. You remember the part that says, "And on his farm he had a wife; with a gimme, gimme, here and a gimme, gimme there, here a gimme, there a gimme, everywhere a gimme, gimme!

Men and women the world over need to be reminded that prayer is not their divine "God gimme" time, rather, it is precious time that you set aside to commune with the Lord. The next step after private devotional prayer is intercessory prayer. Without a doubt this is the kind of supplication that most often moves the hand of God.

Just as God seeks out worshippers that He might bless them, He seeks out those who will be intercessors, that He might bless others. Notice what His Word says:

And I searched for a man among them who would build up the wall and stand in the gap before Me for the land, that I would not destroy it; but I found no one.

EZEKIEL 22:30 NAS

From ancient times, God has looked for and sought to find intercessors, those rare, dedicated individuals who dare to stand in the gap for others.

Moses was an intercessor for the children of Israel. When they made and worshiped the golden calf and God was ready to destroy them, Moses pled for His mercy. (Exodus 32:1-13)

Let's review the four things the Syrophenician woman did and the immediate response she received from the Lord.

She...Came; Knelt; Worshiped and Prayed!

Put those four KEY words in the deepest part of your spirit and remember them, they are your secret to getting an audience with the King!

Until the woman did those four things she received no response whatsoever from the Lord. But look what happened when she, Came; Knelt; Worshiped and Prayed...

And He answered, It is not right (proper, becoming, or fair) to take the children's bread and throw it to the little dogs.

MATTHEW 15:26

While His answer may seem a bit strange to you and me, we must keep in mind that He was sent only to the lost children of the house of Israel. She was asking for something that at that moment was rightfully theirs. Healing and deliverance was all included in the package He brought for God's chosen people.

Never mind what Jesus said to the woman, the important thing is that He answered her.

Remember, **Perseverance** was her **"Powerful Point of Contact!"**

I want you to see that there was absolutely no quitting in this woman. Even though it appeared as if she was rebuffed by the Lord, the Spirit rose up big inside her:

She said,

Yes, Lord, yet even the little pups (little whelps) eat the crumbs that fall from their [young] masters' table.

MATTHEW 15:27

This portion of the story always moves me, especially when I see the way men and women want to give God the crumbs, the left-overs, the last fragments of a day that has been wasted on a myriad of non-essentials.

It's not uncommon for men and women to spend hours glued to the TV screen watching everything from "As the Stomach Turns," to some silly sitcom, to some sporting event that cannot possibly feed the spirit or enlighten the mind. Then, in complete exhaustion as they fall into bed, they ask God to bless, prosper and grant a miracle in their circumstances.

What they are doing is offering God the crumbs of a wasted day or a wasted life. How sad it is to squander even a single hour of the most precious thing God gives us in the natural...TIME! How can anyone expect God's best when the only thing they offer to Him is the crumbs?

The Syrophenician did just the opposite, she offered Christ her best, her complete trust and total worship and then in effect said to Him, "I'm not asking You to take anything that rightfully belongs to the children of Israel and give it to me, just give me a crumb and that will be enough."

Do you understand the significance of what she said to Jesus? Christ told her that deliverance is the children's bread. It is part of God's divine plan, it's included in their inheritance.

She replied, "True and I'm not asking for their portion, just a crumb!" Her faith said, "One small smidgen of Your power is great enough to break the strangle hold the devil has on my daughter." Her testimony was, "It's not the quantity...but the quality of Your presence and power that makes the difference."

In the presence of those who wanted to send her away empty, broken and dejected, this woman exhibited her "Powerful Point of Contact": **Perseverance!**

The simple fact that she would not give in to the pressure of the enemy or give up on the dream of her daughter's deliverance brought this declaration from the Lord:

O woman, great is your faith! Be it done for you as you wish.

MATTHEW 15:28

Don't take the words of Jesus to this woman lightly. The catalyst for her getting a miracle for her troubled daughter was her abiding faith!

It could have been the Canaanite's perseverance that inspired the Apostle Peter to pen this beautiful admonition to the saints of all times:

[You should] be exceedingly glad on this account, though now for a little, you may be distressed by trials and suffer temptations, So that [the genuineness] of your faith may be tested, [your faith] which is infinitely more precious than the perishable gold, which is tested and purified by fire. [This proving of your faith is intended] to redound to [your] praise and glory and honor when Jesus Christ (the Messiah, the Anointed One) is revealed.

1 PETER 1:6-7 AMP

The Syrophenician woman's faith was tried and tested and even though she was buffeted she stayed focused.

Perseverance...her "Powerful Point of Contact" paid great dividends! When she arrived home she found "her daughter was cured..."

Remember it is not your "Point of Contact" that God responds to. Your **"Powerful Point of Contact"** is to help you release your faith for your answer.

The only thing that moves God and produces miracles is...

FAITH!

Section One

Conclusion

The first five chapters of this book are dedicated to raising the level of your faith so that by establishing a "Powerful Point of Contact" you can exercise your faith, for yourself or someone you love to receive an answer from the Lord.

Don't be afraid to venture out in faith and believe God for a special miracle! God has given you dynamic faith, now it is time to use it for His glory.

This is not meant to be an exhaustive study of all the miracles in the Word of God. The sole purpose is to inspire you to approach the Lord with a renewed vision. You are important to Him! He is ready, willing and able to meet all your needs today.

If your "Powerful Point of Contact" takes you into uncharted waters where no one else has gone before, don't be fearful or afraid! Why? Because in the end you will discover a brand new world of answered prayers and dreams fulfilled.

Your faith can never take you beyond God's ability to perform. The more you can believe for, the greater opportunity He has to prove that He:

...is able to do exceeding abundantly above all that we ask or think, according to the power that worketh in us.

Ephesians 3:20 KJV

May your heart say amen to the words of the Apostle Paul:

Unto him be glory in the church by Christ Jesus throughout all ages, world without end. Amen.

EPHESIANS 3:21 KJV

Section Two

Introduction

One of the most crucial aspects of the Christian's life is walking daily, in the will of God.

Throughout this section you will read about men and women who established "Powerful Points of Contact" for personal direction from God that made an impact on everyone around them.

You will learn the secrets of men like David, the illustrious king of Israel, and the Apostle Peter, who, at the lowest point of his life, gained a new sense of direction in the voice of a rooster and proceeded to change his world for Christ.

You will see how a self-willed prophet was so blinded by the desire for money that he didn't recognize a-once-in-a-lifetime miracle when it unfolded right in front of him.

From these you will learn to establish your own "Powerful Point of Contact" for personal direction. You can know the mind of Christ, the will of the Father and the leading of the Holy Spirit.

You are important to God! He is not hiding from you; rather, He is waiting for you to establish a "Powerful Point of Contact" for your miracle. When you do… He will be there in glorious living color to honor your faith.

Section Two

Chapter 6

A Fish Will
Pay The Taxes.

From the dawn of civilization fishing has been a way of life, a means of commerce and a popular pastime among men and women around the globe.

No single sport has more "devotees" world-wide, than that of fishing. Apostles, prophets, priests, presidents, kings, emperors, dictators, senators, statesmen, governors, mayors, policemen, doctors, lawyers, preachers, rabbis, bankers, butchers, bakers, beggars and thieves have, through the centuries, reveled in catching the "Big One."

Wherever you find a lake, pond, river or stream you're likely to find a pole, a net, a trap or a line and an angler trying to outfox a wily bass, trout, salmon or catfish.

Since Adam saw the first silvery creature break water and send ripples to the shore of the Pison River these wonderful creatures from the water-world have captured man's fascination.

Nothing compares to emotional fervor surrounding the fishing industry. Men have fought and nations have gone to war when someone dared to invade another's sacred pools. Some country's base their entire economy on fishing.

But...whoever heard of a fish paying the taxes and what

does it have to do with a "Powerful Point of Contact for Personal Direction?"

Let's see!

Hope springs eternal in the heart of the optimist, or so the saying goes, but there was little hope in Simon Peter's heart, for one more time he had spoken when it would have been better had he remained silent.

Here's the story:

> *And when they came to Capernaum, those who collected the two-drachma tax came to Peter, and said, Does your teacher not pay the two-drachma tax?*
>
> MATTHEW 17:24 NAS

Accosted by the local priests, Peter was asked if Jesus had a current TRS (Temple Revenue Service) statement. Since he didn't want to be "politically incorrect," Peter, cast caution to the wind and said "yes!"

You do understand that I'm being facetious when I say he wanted to be "politically correct?" Neither Jesus nor any of the early day apostles were concerned about "political correctness." They called sin by its proper name whether it was in the kings palace, in the pulpit or the pew.

It wasn't "political correctness" that plagued the apostle in those days rather, that he spoke before thinking and he suffered a terrible lack of intestinal fortitude. Simon was like so many people today who live by the principle of, "Ready...**Fire**...Aim!" On more than one occasion he was guilty of speaking or acting before thinking and who can forget the way he cowardly denied that he was a disciple or that he even knew Christ.

Isn't it wonderful that we have a Savior Who, after we

make a terrible decision, can turn it into a positive learning experience? That's what Jesus did in this instance!

Before Peter could broach the subject, Jesus opened the conversation by asking the question:

What do you think, Simon? From whom do the kings of the earth collect customs or poll-tax, from their sons or from strangers?

MATTHEW 17:25 NAS

For clarity sake, let me explain the tax the priests were collecting. This was first imposed on the Israeli soldiers in the days of Moses, (Exodus 30:13-16) it was a ransom each man paid when going to war.

The word "ransom" used here refers to money paid by one who is guilty of taking human life in circumstances that do not constitute murder. A soldier who marched into battle was in the eyes of Heaven a potential taker of life, though not a deliberate murderer. Therefore he required a ransom for his life.

Keep that thought in mind, because it will make the words of Christ more meaningful.

Some people read the Old Testament with a mindset that God sent His people on senseless killing rampages, but that is not true. God is and has always been full of love and mercy. The thought of anyone being killed, even in war, grieves His heart. Thus God instituted the ransom for the soldier going to war.

By Christ's time the original use and meaning was long forgotten, rather than being a ransom for men going to war, it had become a way to raise funds to repair the temple.

No wonder Jesus considered Himself exempt. He knew the true meaning and purpose for the tax was to be a ransom. He did not need to pay a ransom tax since His mission in life, His sole purpose for coming into the world was to be the sacrificial Lamb.

He was not a killer...He is the Giver of life!

Don't allow the tax issue to cloud your thoughts, this is not about whether it's right or not to pay taxes, rather, it is a lesson in identity. Christ used this opportunity to state His position as the Redeemer, the One who paid the true ransom for all mankind.

When Jesus asked, *"From whom do the kings of the earth collect customs or poll-tax, from their sons or from strangers?"*

Peter correctly answered *"From strangers,"* to which Jesus responded, *"Consequently the sons are exempt."*

Jesus in truth said to Peter, *"My Father is the eternal God of heaven. Since I am His only begotten Son and not a stranger, through divine Sonship I am exempt from paying the tax."*

The Lord had every right not to pay the temple tax, but He didn't exercise those rights, instead, He said:

> *However, so that we do not offend them, go to the sea and throw in a hook, and take the first fish that comes up; and when you open its mouth you will find a shekel. Take that and give it to them for you and Me.*

MATTHEW 17: 27 NAS

Christ's directive to Simon Peter is amusing, notice what He said; *"go to the sea and throw in a hook, and take the first fish that comes up."* Why did the Lord specifically say, "take the first fish," when Peter only needed one coin to pay the taxes?

He no doubt knew that the old fisherman nature was alive and well in Simon and when he got started fishing he wouldn't want to stop with just one fish?

When you read the New Testament it is easy to think that Peter, James and John were the Lord's favorites. They were with Him at all times. They were the only ones that accompanied Him to the Mount of Transfiguration. They were allowed to go with Him to Jairus' house where He raised the little girl from the dead. And on the night He was betrayed they were called apart from the other disciples in the Garden of Gethsemane.

Did that mean they were more special or that He loved them more than Andrew, Matthew, Nathaniel, Simon the Zealot, Bartholomew or the rest?

I seriously doubt that Jesus loved Peter, James and John any more than anyone else!

When I was a boy my school teachers had me sitting on the front row near their desk, it wasn't because they especially liked me, but that it was easier to control me in the front than in the back of the classroom.

People think Peter, James and John were always near Jesus because they were special. Could it have been that Jesus had them close to Him so He could keep track of what they were doing?

One man said the Lord gave Peter the keys to the Kingdom so that when they rattled He knew where he was.

Jesus taught Simon Peter a lesson in specifics to help him establish a "Powerful Point of Contact" for personal direction! He gave him five distinct things to do:

1. "Go to the sea!" To those who have never been to Israel this may seem the only logical place for Simon to go fish, but if you've been there you realize he could have gone to the Jordan River to the north where it feeds into the Sea of Galilee or to the south where the river flows out of the sea. I love the manner in which the Lord uses specificity! When He says "go to the sea," the sea is where you begin your journey of faith!

2. "Throw in a hook," again, notice the exactness of

Christ's instruction! This is the same man that He told:

*...Launch out into the deep, and let down your **nets** for a draught. And Simon answering said unto him, Master, we have toiled all the night, and have taken nothing: nevertheless at thy word I will let down the **net**. And when they had this done, they inclosed a great multitude of fishes: and their **net** brake. And they beckoned unto their partners, which were in the other ship, that they should come and help them. And they came, and filled both the ships, so that they began to sink. When Simon Peter saw it, he fell down at Jesus' knees, saying, Depart from me; for I am a sinful man, O Lord. For he was astonished, and all that were with him, at the draught of the fishes which they had taken:*

Luke 5:4-9KJV

On that occasion Jesus told them to let down their **nets** but, Peter, thinking he knew more about fishing than Jesus did, let down a **net**. Obviously the Lord knew what He was talking about, because the **net** began to break. When Jesus speaks He is precise so if He says **nets**, don't make the mistake of letting down a **net**!

"Throw in a hook," there was no need for a net this time since only one fish was necessary.

Just as God had a prophet-collecting-whale in the Old Testament waiting to catch Jonah, He had a coin-collector fish in the New Testament waiting for Simon to catch it.

3. "Take the first fish that comes up!" In all likelihood the first fish was a scavenger and according to the law it was unclean. It was certainly not the kind of fish Peter liked to catch, it wasn't good for food but...it was great for paying the tax bill! Knowing that Peter would remove it from the hook and throw it back, Jesus told him exactly what to do.

4. "Open its mouth you will find a shekel." I never cease to marvel at God's wondrous ability, His divine knowledge and the manner with which He accomplishes His perfect will. Think with me for a moment of everything that had to happen to make this miracle fall into place.

Someone needed to lose a coin, even though in actuality it wasn't lost, rather, it was an investment in a miracle. God marked the exact place the coin came to rest at the bottom of the sea and when the time was right He aroused the curiosity of a certain fish.

While Jesus was telling Simon Peter to go fishing, He was also speaking to the fish to retrieve the coin and be first in line to grab the hook.

There are some people who would say the entire chain of events were purely coincidental, but those of us who have faith in God see the hand of the Lord working from start to finish.

5. "Take that and give it to them for you and Me." It is so important for each of us to follow the directions of the Lord explicitly. At no point in this account was there room for error if Peter did what Jesus told him to do.

It was not the value of the shekel that makes this story so fascinating, but the lesson Christ taught His disciple on listening to His words and obeying them. Simon Peter's *"Powerful Point of Contact"* for personal direction was "HEARING!"

As an example of a Rhema from God and how I obeyed His voice, let me share a wonderful story with you.

In 1964 I was on my way to Kampala, Uganda, for our first great African Crusade. Because there were no connecting flights, we had to stay overnight in London, England.

When I got to my hotel room I began to seek the face of the Lord and I felt a stirring in my spirit. I must admit I didn't like what I was feeling and I remember saying, "God, please, don't send me to Great Britain, I don't ever want to come here."

Several years before I had preached in some Assemblies of God Churches in England and to me they were stuffy and cold.

As I prayed in that little hotel room I knew that despite all my objections and protesting, the Holy Spirit was quickening something in the depths of my soul.

The next morning we continued our journey to Africa without realizing that God had a plan far bigger than anything I had ever imagined.

One day after a great miracle service, a short, stocky, white man came out of the crowd and asked to have a word with me. As we talked he told me that God had sent him from Great Britain to tell me that I was to go to London for a crusade.

My first impulse was to say, "I've already told the Lord that I don't want to go to England because the people are cold, aloof and stuffy." But the Holy Spirit prompted me to hold my peace and listen to the servant of God.

You see, the man really was sent by the Lord and his message to me was directly from the throne. God wanted me to look at Great Britain through His eyes and not my own. God wanted to use me to open up that nation to His saving grace and miracle working power.

The following year we went to England for the great London Deeper Life Crusade and I have returned every year since.

As a result of our obedience to go to Great Britain, God has opened many other nations in Europe to the Gospel.

I was guilty of looking at that wonderful nation through the eyes of man, not through the eyes of the Holy Spirit. The feeling of aloofness was a trick of the devil to keep me from going there and winning thousands to Christ.

Some of this ministry's most dedicated partners are from the very place I told God I didn't ever want to go. How sad it would have been not to hear the voice of God.

Before you act...you must hear!
When you hear...you must act!

One of the classic examples of Christ's words being the "Powerful Point of Contact" for personal direction is the story of Jesus turning water into wine.

Let's see what the Bible says:

On the third day there was a wedding in Cana of Galilee, and the mother of Jesus was there. Now both Jesus and His disciples were invited to the wedding. And when they ran out of wine, the mother of Jesus said to Him, "They have no wine." Jesus said to her, "Woman, what does your concern have to do with Me? My hour has not yet come." His mother said to the servants, "Whatever He says to you, do it." Now there were set there six waterpots of stone, according to the manner of purification of the Jews, containing twenty or thirty gallons apiece. Jesus said to them, "Fill the waterpots with water." And they filled them up to the brim. And He said to them, "Draw some out now, and take it to the master of the feast." And they took it. When the master of the feast had tasted the water that was made wine, and did not know where it came from (but the servants who had drawn the water knew), the master of the feast called the bridegroom. And he said to him, "Every man at the beginning sets out the good wine, and when the guests have well drunk, then the inferior. You have kept the good wine until now!" This beginning of signs Jesus did in Cana of Galilee, and manifested His glory; and His disciples believed in Him.

JOHN 2: 1-12 NKJ

There are some very salient points that emphasize the

necessity of hearing and obeying the Lord in this intriguing story.

This beautiful account will act as a roadmap for anyone who wants to establish a "Powerful Point of Contact" with God for personal direction.

When the wedding feast ran out of wine the mother of Jesus came to him to solve the problem, but when she did, He said, *"Woman, what does your concern have to do with Me? My hour has not yet come."*

Mary then turned to the servants and said, *"Whatever He says to you, do it."* This lesson is of vital importance to everyone who wants to be blessed of God.

Each time I read this portion of Scripture I am impressed with the action of the servants. When Jesus said, *"Fill the waterpots with water."* The Bible says, *"they filled them up to the brim."*

If you want to accomplish great things for God it is vital that you learn the value of going all out for Him. When He tells you to fill waterpots, always...always...always fill them up to the brim. Never leave any doubt that you are fully committed to Him.

As soon as the servants returned with the full-to-the-brim waterpots, Jesus said, *"Draw some out now, and take it to the master of the feast."*

Can you imagine the thrill those servants received as they participated in one of the greatest miracles of all time? They knew they had filled the waterpots with fresh cool water, but somewhere between the well and the wedding the crystal clear water turned into red vintage wine. Then they were given the privilege of serving it to the master of the feast.

Turning the water into wine was no chore for Jesus, all He needed was some faithful servants who would hear His words and fill the waterpots.

Simon Peter and the servants discovered the secret to establishing a "Powerful Point of Contact," for personal direction is in hearing the voice of God and obeying!

If you want to see the miracles of God performed in your life... if you want to do great exploits in His name, it is crucial that you establish a "Powerful Point of Contact," for personal direction.

Remember!

Before you act...you must hear!

When you hear...you must act!

Section Two

Chapter 7
Stop...Look...Listen!

Regardless of how many times you have waged warfare with the devil you must continually rely on divine guidance, to do otherwise will result in tragedy and defeat.

David, king of Israel, is a prime example of what it means to seek the face of God for a "Powerful Point of Contact" for personal direction before going to battle against the forces of darkness.

From the moment he stepped on the battlefield against Goliath, the Philistine giant, David was never the same. In a split second he went from a youthful shepherd boy to the most courageous soldier Israel had ever seen.

As a shepherd, David established a personal relationship with God. He learned that God is a very present help in times of need. Whether it was protecting his father's flock from natural predators or fighting against the enemies of his people, Israel, David called on God for divine direction.

On the lonely Judean hillsides David prepared himself mentally, physically and spiritually to go to war against the Philistines or anyone else who sought to harm the chosen race.

The battle against the Philistines and the giant Goliath was the defining moment of David's life. For forty days Goliath hurled insults at Israel and spoke blasphemously against Almighty God. Neither King Saul, David's three eldest brothers

Eliab, Shammah or Abinadab, nor anyone else in the Israeli army was brave enough to confront the loud mouth giant. No one...that is, until David the shepherd boy came on the scene.

I find it very interesting that so little is said about David's seven brothers other than mentioning that the three eldest were in Saul's army. Even those three failed to carve out a place of prominence in Bible history.

Could it have been that they all lacked the desire to search out and find their own "Powerful Point of Contact" for personal direction from God?

There was a major contrast between David and his three brothers, for forty days they listened to the insults of Goliath and did nothing. The shepherd boy needed to hear the foul-mouth, over-grown Philistine only once to raise his righteous indignation.

David was not one to stand idly by and let anyone curse his God or speak derogatorily against His chosen people. He had the courage to stand up and fight for God and country.

Here is the Biblical account of what happened that day:

> *Now the Philistines gathered their forces for war and assembled at Socoh in Judah. They pitched camp at Ephes Dammim, between Socoh and Azekah. Saul and the Israelites assembled and camped in the Valley of Elah and drew up their battle line to meet the Philistines. The Philistines occupied one hill and the Israelites another, with the valley between them. A champion named Goliath, who was from Gath, came out of the Philistine camp. He was over nine feet tall... Goliath stood and shouted to the ranks of Israel, Why do you come out and line up for battle? Am I not a Philistine, and are you not the servants of Saul? Choose a man and have him come down to me. If he is able to fight and kill me, we will become your subjects; but if I*

overcome him and kill him, you will become our subjects and serve us. Then the Philistine said, This day I defy the ranks of Israel! Give me a man and let us fight each other. On hearing the Philistine's words, Saul and all the Israelites were dismayed and terrified... Jesse's three oldest sons had followed Saul to the war: The firstborn was Eliab; the second, Abinadab; and the third, Shammah. David was the youngest. For forty days the Philistine came forward every morning and evening and took his stand. Now Jesse said to his son David, Take this ephah of roasted grain and these ten loaves of bread for your brothers and hurry to their camp. Take along these ten cheeses to the commander of their unit. See how your brothers are and bring back some assurance from them. They are with Saul and all the men of Israel in the Valley of Elah, fighting against the Philistines. Early in the morning David left the flock with a shepherd, loaded up and set out, as Jesse had directed. He reached the camp as the army was going out to its battle positions, shouting the war cry. Israel and the Philistines were drawing up their lines facing each other. David left his things with the keeper of supplies, ran to the battle lines and greeted his brothers. As he was talking with them, Goliath, the Philistine champion from Gath, stepped out from his lines and shouted his usual defiance, and David heard it. When the Israelites saw the man, they all ran from him in great fear... David said to Saul, Let no one lose heart on account of this Philistine; your servant will go and fight him. Saul replied, You are not able to go out against this Philistine and fight him; you are only a boy, and he has been a fighting man from his youth. But David said to Saul, Your servant has been keeping his father's sheep. When a lion or a bear came and carried off a sheep from the flock, I went after it, struck it and rescued the sheep from its mouth. When it turned on me, I seized it by its hair, struck it and killed it. Your servant has killed both the lion and the bear; this uncircumcised Philistine will be like one of them, because he has defied the armies of the living God. The LORD who delivered me from the paw of the lion and the paw of the bear will deliver me from the hand of this Philistine. Saul said to David, Go, and the LORD be with you. Then he took his staff in his hand, chose five smooth stones from the stream, put them in the pouch of his shepherd's bag and, with his sling in his hand, approached the Philistine. Meanwhile, the Philistine, with his shield bearer in front of him, kept coming closer to David. He looked David over and saw that he was only a boy, ruddy and handsome, and he despised him. He said to David, Am I a dog, that you come at me with sticks? And the Philistine cursed David by his gods. Come here, he said, and I'll give your flesh to the birds of the air and the beasts of the field! David said to the Philistine, You come against me with sword and spear and javelin, but I come against you in the name of the LORD ALMIGHTY, the God of the armies of Israel, whom you have defied. This day the LORD will hand you over to me, and I'll strike you down and cut off your head. Today I will give the carcasses of the Philistine army to the birds of the air and the beasts of the earth, and the whole world will know that there is a God in Israel. All those gathered here will know that it is not by sword or spear that the LORD saves; for the battle is the LORD's, and he will give all of you into our hands. As the Philistine moved closer to attack him, David ran quickly toward the battle line to meet him. Reaching into his bag and taking out a stone, he slung it and struck the Philistine on the forehead. The stone sank into his forehead, and he fell facedown on the ground. So David triumphed over the Philistine with a sling and a stone; without a sword in his hand he struck down the

Philistine and killed him. David ran and stood over him. He took hold of the Philistine's sword and drew it from the scabbard. After he killed him, he cut off his head with the sword.

I SAMUEL 17:1-51(EDITED) NIV

Did you notice that when he spoke to King Saul, David gave credit to God for protecting him? He recognized that for him to prevail against his foes he needed help and divine guidance from the Lord.

In the beginning David fought wild beasts and the elements of nature to protect his father Jesse's sheep, but as the anointed king, he battled against the Philistines and other nations to protect Israel, his Father Jehovah's sheep.

Throughout his reign as king of Israel and Judah, David continued to seek the face of God to receive the "Powerful Point of Contact" for personal direction for each new encounter. He never took for granted that the instructions he received for the last battle were sufficient for the one at hand.

Let me give you some examples of the way David sought the face of God for his "Powerful Point of Contact" for personal direction.

Now the Philistines came and spread themselves out in the valley of Rephaim. Then David inquired of the LORD, saying, Shall I go up against the Philistines? Wilt Thou give them into my hand? And the LORD said to David, Go up, for I will certainly give the Philistines into your hand. So David came to Baal-perazim, and defeated them there; and he said, The LORD has broken through my enemies before me like the breakthrough of waters...

II SAMUEL 5:18-20 NAS

David received a divine "Breakthrough," when he established a "Powerful Point of Contact" for personal direction from the Lord. He didn't go into battle relying on his own wisdom or understanding, rather, he waited until he heard from God.

One of the greatest mistakes men and women ever make is rushing into battle with the forces of darkness without a clear directive from God. When anyone enters into spiritual warfare it must be in the strength of the Lord if they expect to win.

David distinguished himself as a mighty warrior when he dared to go out against Goliath. He was fearless, because he knew the great Shepherd of Israel was on the battlefield with him. He recognized that it was not in his strength. He knew that it was not by his own power that he would destroy the giant, but through the power, the might and the strength of God.

The intriguing thing about this great man is that nothing deterred him from his pursuit of God. As a shepherd boy, as a soldier in Saul's army, as a fugitive from Saul and as the king of Israel he sought the face of the Lord for a "Powerful Point of Contact" for personal direction.

In the Scriptures above we read how David called on God for guidance when the Philistines set themselves in battle array in the valley of Rephaim. And we also saw how the army of Israel routed the enemy when they waited for a word from God.

If David had been like a lot of people, when the Philistines came back to the same place he defeated them before he would have marched out against them without giving it a second thought.

Common sense should tell you that if you trounce the enemy once you can surely do it again! But when you are fighting against the powers of darkness you need more than common sense...you need a definite word from God... you need a "Powerful Point of Contact" for personal direction!

David could not afford to enter even one battle without consulting God and knowing His perfect will. The lives of his men and the future of the nation were at stake. So, when the Philistines came to the valley of Rephaim again, just like before, he set his face to seek the Lord.

Notice what the Word says:

> *Now the Philistines came up once again and spread themselves out in the valley of Rephaim. And when David inquired of the LORD, He said, You shall not go directly up; circle around behind them and come at them in front of the balsam trees. And it shall be, when you hear the sound of marching in the tops of the balsam trees, then you shall act promptly, for then the LORD will have gone out before you to strike the army of the Philistines. Then David did so, just as the LORD had commanded him, and struck down the Philistines from Geba as far as Gezer.*
>
> II SAMUEL 5:22-25 NAS

I cannot over-emphasize the importance of having a divine directive from God when you encounter the devil. If David the great warrior king needed to have a word from God when he fought against the Philistines, you and I certainly need one today.

I wonder how many times David had to hold the Israeli army back while he waited for the Holy Spirit to blow through the leaves of the balsam trees?

Knowing human nature as I do, and how impatient mankind is, I'm sure he had to hold a tight rein on them or they would have dashed out on the battlefield without the protection of their Commander in Chief.

No doubt Joab, the commander of the army, wanted to rush into battle especially after the Lord revealed His strategic plan to them. Logic would have it that the Israeli army needed to strike quickly before the Philistines discovered where they were.

Logic, however, does not figure into the equation when you have a "Rhema," an inspired word from God.

When you establish a "Powerful Point of Contact" for personal direction, nothing should sway your thinking. You should pursue the desired objective with reckless abandon.

We must not overlook one of the most crucial statements God said to David when He gave him battle instructions.

Notice what He said:

> *And it shall be, when you hear the sound of marching in the tops of the balsam trees, **then you shall act promptly,***

Too many people fail to act promptly when the Holy Spirit speaks and it leaves them vulnerable to the attacks of the enemy.

I urge my family, partners and friends to obey God quickly when He speaks, because the reward for obedience is always beyond human imagination.

Prompt action leads to success, while the failure to act opens the door to doubt, frustration and defeat.

Let's look at what God promised He would do when David and the Israeli army acted promptly:

> *...for then the LORD will have gone out before you to strike the army of the Philistines.*

I must call your attention to the sentence structure of God's promise. God said when you are acting so is He. Look at the way He said it: *"...for then the LORD will have gone out before you!"*

Do you see it? The moment you act on the divine directive, and obey the instructions of God, you have His promise that He has already gone before you to defeat your enemy.

Here's the wonderful part!

It doesn't matter if your enemy is sickness, disease, pain, heartache, marital problems, drugs, alcohol, tobacco or financial difficulties. When you establish a "Powerful Point of Contact" for personal direction, and you have a Word, a Rhema, a divine revelation from God...**and you act promptly**...God will go before you to perform miracles on your behalf. That's His promise to you!

The Lord is looking for men and women who will STOP what they are doing, LOOK beyond their circumstances, their problems and their limitations and LISTEN to the Holy Spirit.

Let me explain what I mean by

STOP, LOOK and LISTEN!

We live in a society that is in a hurry. Everything we do, we want to do faster than it has ever been done before.

Restaurants have drive-thru fast food, pharmacies have drive-thru windows and banks have drive-thru tellers. This is so you can do your banking, eat the burger you bought at the drive-thru restaurant and take the medicine you picked up at the drive-thru drug store while you listen to your favorite CD, talk on your cell phone and play a video game on your micro-computer.

Then we wonder why it's so hard to establish a "Powerful Point of Contact" for personal direction. If any man or woman wants to have a relationship with God, they must **STOP** what they are doing and seek His face.

Second, it is imperative that you **LOOK** beyond your own natural abilities. If you desire a supernatural visitation then you must look up. If you spend your life walking in the flesh and fulfilling your carnal appetites you will never enjoy the sweetness of fellowship your spirit craves.

It's time to open your eyes and **LOOK** at all the good

things God has prepared for you. Look beyond the natural to the supernatural where His glory awaits you!

And third... *LISTEN!*

What are you listening to? Do you feed your heart and soul on the everlasting promises of God or do you starve the inner man by flooding your ears with the unwholesome, unholy, ungodly garbage the world spews out?

If your radio dial is set for filthy rap, godless rock or tear jerking country music, your spirit will languish.

If you have your TV set on the Sad Sally Show or Mindless Donohue or some silly soap you can rest assured that God will not break through the sound barrier you have raised up and speak His revelation to your heart.

You must listen for Him!

Listen...as if He only spoke in a still small voice! **Listen...** for His words will still the storm and calm your troubled sea. He will speak peace...but you must...**Listen!**

You can establish a "Powerful Point of Contact" for personal direction when you **STOP – LOOK – LISTEN!**

Section Two

Chapter 8
The Donkey That Didn't Talk

One of the strangest events that ever took place on earth was when Balaam's donkey spoke to the angry prophet with a human voice.

Sound impossible? Let's see!

The children of Israel were in the final stages of their forty year trek across the desert. As they approached the Promised Land they passed near the territory of Moab.

Fearful that they would invade his country, Balak, king of Moab summoned the prophet Balaam to come and place a curse on the children of God.

As soon as Balaam received word from the king to come curse Israel he enquired of God whether he should go. God spoke to him emphatically that he was not to go.

Rebuffed by the prophet, the king sent higher ranking dignitaries with a more handsome reward for his services.

Had Balaam been a man of honor and dignity he would never have entertained the second group of visitors. But the spirit of greed and the lust for power reduced him to the likeness of those who wanted to cast a curse on Israel.

God's first adamant answer should have convinced Balaam that He would not change His mind and that he should get on with his life. But... Balaam wouldn't take no for an answer and when he was given conditional permission he gladly followed the ambassadors Balak sent to him.

While on his way to meet the heathen king, Balaam encountered an angel. The sad part was that by the time he was in the angel's presence he was so blinded by greed and his personal desire that he didn't see him.

It was to his benefit that the donkey he was riding saw the angel with his sword drawn and turned out of the path to keep her master from suffering certain death.

Angry that she had turned aside, Balaam hit her with a stick and drove her back to the path. Again the donkey saw the angel poised and ready to wreak havoc on the disobedient prophet, so she crushed his leg against a wall and again the prophet struck her with his stick.

The next time the donkey saw the angel there was nothing she could do except lie down. The prophet was so angry that he hit her again with the stick. At this point the donkey said to him:

"What have I done to you that you have struck me these three times?" Numbers 22:28 NAS

It's hard to fathom the prophet being so angry that he failed to realize the phenomena that had taken place. Rather than shaking his head in amazement, he carried on a conversation with her.

Balaam said:

Because you have made a mockery of me! If there had been a sword in my hand I would have killed you by now.
NUMBERS 22:29 NAS

Imagine how comical that must have been to the donkey, the prophet was on his way to curse the people of God with nothing but words, but he needed a sword to kill her!

The conversation continued with the donkey saying: *"Am I not your donkey on which you have ridden all your life to this day? Have I ever been accustomed to do so to you?"* And he said "No."

Then the Lord opened the prophet's eyes. When he saw the angel standing with his sword drawn Balaam fell on his face. You struck your donkey three times and threatened to kill her for saving your life the angel said.

I wouldn't be surprised if he said, you ought to hug her neck and kiss her because if she had been as dumb as you are, you'd be dead by now.

If the prophet had been looking for a, "Powerful Point of Contact," for personal direction from God, he would have surely recognized it in this supernatural encounter, but he wasn't. All he wanted was the reward the king had promised.

God allowed Balaam to continue his journey!

Some people seem to think God sanctions what they are doing simply because He doesn't kill them or at least stop them by some miraculous means.

That God allowed Balaam to continue his journey didn't mean He approved, it meant that God had given the prophet the power of choice and that He would allow him to disobey.

It is to our advantage to remember that choices, good or bad, always have consequences!

Was Balaam a true prophet or just a sorcerer from the land of the Chaldees? That question has been argued by priests, preachers and rabbis for hundreds of years.

Through the ages many rabbis seem to agree that during this particular time in his life Balaam received a revelation from God about Israel and that he spoke with divine unction from above when he described the children of God and their future prowess as a nation.

From the wayward prophet's lips flowed some of the most beautiful phrases of praise to God and his description of Israel has brought joy to the hearts of men for centuries.

King Balak hired him to use black magic, incantations and enchantments to conjure up a curse on the chosen people, but when he stood high on a mountain and saw Israel spread out in the valley below, all that came from his mouth were words of acclaim.

Israel was not just another disorganized nomadic tribe littering the desert. When Balaam looked at the camp the sight before his eyes was breathtaking.

I want you to grasp this magnificent picture...

The majestic Tabernacle of Witness stood in the center of the camp, overshadowed by a pillar of a cloud. The tabernacle was erected due East and West, so it received the first rays of the rising sun and the last rays of the setting sun.

The twelve tribes formed a circle around the tabernacle. Each tribe had its beautiful banners flying in the desert breeze. But even more impressive was the way each tent was set up.

The doorway of each tent faced the tabernacle, so that when the father brought his family inside each night and turned to fasten the tent flap, the last thing he saw was the Tabernacle of the Lord with the pillar of fire glowing above it.

Likewise in the morning when he arose and opened the door the first thing he saw was the place of worship and the glory cloud that covered it.

It was this scene that inspired Balaam to exclaim:

> *God is not a man, that he should lie; neither the son of man that he should repent: hath he said, and shall he not do it? or hath he spoken, and shall he not make it good? Behold, I have received commandment to bless:*

and he hath blessed; and I cannot reverse it.

NUMBERS 23:19-20 KJV

Wow! It's no wonder that Israel felt they could conquer the land... morning and night they were encompassed with the presence of the mighty God of Heaven. They lived with the wonderful assurance that they were the apple of His eye.

The inscription on Balaam's grave stone should have read:

"Missed Opportunity!"

Had the perverse prophet been looking for a "Powerful Point of Contact" for personal direction from God he would have certainly found it when his faithful donkey spoke to him. And... yes! According to the New Testament, the donkey really did speak with a human voice:

Balaam was stopped from his mad course when his donkey spoke to him with a human voice, scolding and rebuking him. II PETER 2:16 TLB

Never again in the history of the world is there a record of a donkey speaking with the voice of a man, but the annals of time are littered with instances where men have reversed that role and what they said sounded like a donkey braying.

The New Testament gives a totally different scenario. In this instance, another donkey plays a major role, this time, even though it doesn't speak, it serves as "Powerful Point of Contact" for personal direction to Christ's disciples.

Knowing that the days of His earthly life were quickly drawing to a close, the Lord taught His followers to establish "Powerful Points of Contact" so their faith would not be shaken when persecution came against them.

Jesus had no misgivings about dying; that was His reason for coming into the world! The disciples, however, needed something to sustain them, something tangible to hold to after

He was gone.

It was with this purpose in mind that He taught them to establish, *"Powerful Points of Contact,"* for personal direction. He used a variety of things, including a rooster and a donkey, to help them recognize that even in the face of death, He was in control.

The Bible gives us this story about the Lord and His disciples prior to His triumphal entry into the city:

> *And when they had approached Jerusalem and had come to Bethphage, to the Mount of Olives, then Jesus sent two disciples, saying to them, Go into the village opposite you, and immediately you will find a donkey tied there and a colt with her; untie them and bring them to me. If anyone says anything to you, you shall say, The Lord has need of them, and immediately he will send them. Now this took place to fulfill what was spoken through the prophet: SAY TO THE DAUGHTER OF ZION, BEHOLD YOUR KING IS COMING TO YOU, GENTLE, AND MOUNTED ON A DONKEY, EVEN A COLT, THE FOAL OF A BEAST OF BURDEN. The disciples went and did just as Jesus had instructed them, and brought the donkey and the colt, and laid their coats on them, and He sat on the coats.*
>
> MATTHEW 21:1-7 NAS

This incident was extremely important, because it fulfilled the prophecy of Zechariah 9:9. It not only fulfilled the prophecy given hundreds of years before, it helped the two disciples to establish a "Powerful Point of Contact," for personal direction.

The moment they saw the donkey tied with the foal beside her, their faith had a definite point of reference. They knew they could rely on the word of Christ, because everything was as He said it would be.

Balaam's donkey talked to him with a human voice, but the infuriated prophet was so intent on receiving man's reward he never realized it was a miracle. Had he been seeking God for a "Powerful Point of Contact" for personal direction, his faith would have been strengthened immeasurably.

In the New Testament the donkeys didn't need to talk, the fact that they were where Jesus said they would be was enough for the disciples to establish a "Powerful Point of Contact!"

A few days later Jesus used another unlikely creature to help Simon Peter find his way back after he had denied three times that he even knew the Lord.

Having finished supper they went to the Mount of Olives:

> *Then Jesus said to them, All of you will be made to stumble because of Me this night, for it is written: I will smite the Shepard and the sheep of the flock will be scattered. But after I have been raised, I will go before you to Galilee.*

Not wanting to be one to deny the Lord:

> *Peter answered and said to Him, Even if all are made to stumble because of You, I will never be made to stumble.*

I'm certain Simon Peter was sincere when he made this hasty assertion but the Lord knew something about him that even he did not know, that's why he answered him in this manner:

Jesus said to him,
> *Assuredly I say to you that this night, before the rooster crows, you will deny Me three times. Peter said to Him, Even if I have to die with You, I will not deny You!*

MATTHEW 26:31-35

When Jesus told Peter that he would deny Him three times before the rooster crowed He was establishing a "Powerful Point of Contact," for personal direction. He was saying to Simon, "When you hear the rooster crow, remember that I love you and I'm watching out for you."

You already know the rest of the story, in a few hours the mob came to the Garden of Gethsemane, Judas betrayed Jesus with a kiss and the chief priests had Him arrested.

Seeing the howling mob about to take the Lord, Peter drew his sword and started swinging wildly. Seeking to inflict major damage he managed to get close enough to a servant of the high priest that he cut the man's ear off.

To Simon's sheer amazement, the Lord touched the wounded man and made him whole, but even that miracle didn't change the attitude of the mob. They arrested the Lord and led Him away to the high priest.

Once inside the compound the servant girl who kept the door said to Peter,

> *You are not also one of this Man's disciples, are you? He said, I am not.*
>
> John 18:17 NKJ

A little later, while warming himself by a fire of coals the soldiers had built, Peter could have consoled himself that he had indeed stood up for the Lord, after all, no one else drew a sword in His defense.

Then someone else said,

> *You are not also one of His disciples, are you? He denied it and said, I am not!*
>
> John 18:25

But wait, the questioning was not over, remember the Lord said he would deny Him three times.

> *One of the servants of the high priest, a relative of*

him whose ear Peter cut off, said, Did I not see you in the garden with Him? Peter then denied again; and immediately a rooster crowed.

JOHN 18:26-27 NKJ

John's Gospel treats Peter's denial of the Lord gentler than Matthew and Mark, perhaps it's because John was closer to him and knew the anguish he suffered for his vehement words against Christ. The other Gospels state that Peter not only denied him, but that he also uttered a curse against the Savior.

Luke's Gospel says:

...Immediately while he was still speaking, the rooster crowed. And the Lord turned and looked at Peter. Then he remembered the word of the Lord, how He said to him, Before the rooster crows, you will deny me three times. So Peter went out and wept bitterly.

LUKE 22:60-62 NKJ

Do you see and understand what I am teaching? Jesus used a donkey to help two of His disciples establish a "Powerful Point of Contact" for personal direction.

For Simon Peter, He used a rooster! In another place he used a fig tree. Through these objects and creatures He taught His disciples to lean heavily on His word.

You can establish a **"Powerful Point of Contact"** for **personal direction**, by taking hold of the words He spoke in Bible times and the Rhema Word He gives to you today.

Remember what Jesus said:

Heaven and earth will pass away, but My words shall not pass away.

MATTHEW 24:35 NAS

There is not a more, **"Powerful Point of Contact"** for **personal direction** in the world than the Word of God!

111

Section Two

Chapter 9
He Really Is A Know-It-All

L ife was at best... boring! She had tried to be a good wife, but each time she got married things went wrong and ended up in divorce. Sad, lonely, discouraged and downcast she made her daily trip to the town watering hole.

To say that she made the trip hoping to find someone interesting would have been a stretch of one's imagination. She had given up any thoughts of finding a decent man since her reputation had long since branded her as a person of ill repute.

Occasionally, she would go when the local ladies society was meeting just to spice up their gossip sessions, but most of the time she went when no one was there. That way she didn't have to answer questions and she didn't have to feel the contemptuous gaze of the "do-gooders."

Most of the women in the community regarded her as the "Rahab" of the area and refused to have anything to do with her, as if they could somehow be soiled simply by association.

When she arrived on that particular day she noticed a foreigner sitting alone, in deep contemplation. Perhaps he was weary from his journey or maybe... no, she wouldn't allow herself to even think he had come to see her.

While this was not a place exclusively for the

townswomen, men seldom came there unless their thirst got the best of them or they were looking for someone.

"Forget it," she said to herself, "get your jug filled and go on back home so you can drink in the solitude of your own place without the whispers of the uppity old women."

Suddenly, the stranger broke the silence!

"Give me a drink!" he said.

Now that was a unique approach, she thought.

Does this foreigner honestly think he can con me into sharing my precious liquid with him? Doesn't he realize what I had to do to get my jug filled at this place?

Wait... there was something vaguely familiar about this foreigner. Then she remembered, he was from a neighboring country and they had no time for each other.

"Why are you asking me for a drink, you know my country and yours have no dealings with each other?" she asked.

"If you knew who I am and what I have to offer, you would have asked me for a drink!" the stranger replied.

"I don't see your jug, so how could you give me a drink even if I asked? If you have something that good, where did you get it? And what makes you think that it's better than what we have here?"

"It's the quality of what I'm offering that makes mine superior to yours. You've been coming here every day for years, the more you drink the more you need. You never really get satisfied. You can drink and drink, but you always feel empty inside, as if you've not had anything at all."

One drink from me and you feel as if you have a fountain bubbling inside you. You'll never want to come back here again.

114

What an offer!

She questioned in her heart, can this stranger really giv me something to drink that's so wonderful I'll never have to come here again? Never have to frequent this old watering hole where the town gossips gather and never have to hear their whispers behind my back?

"Stranger, I've finished off many a jug from this place, but if you've got something even half as good as you say, I want to try it! I'll take you up on your offer, give me a drink."

"Before I serve your drink," the man said, "Go get your husband."

"I don't have a husband!" she exclaimed.

"You don't have a husband? You've had five husbands! After the fifth one you decided there was no advantage to being married and now you just let them move in for as long as the two of you can stand each other!" The stranger said.

A thousand thoughts raced through the woman's mind, who was this man? How did he know so much about her? Was he some kind of traveling soothsayer? What could he possibly want from her? Maybe he is a prophet! That's it, the man is a prophet!

"Mister, I'm beginning to think you're a prophet of some kind. I'm not against religion, but you see we have our own way of praying to God and I'm quite sure it's different from yours.

Our father's worshiped in this mountain… Worship! That's the word the Stranger had been waiting to hear! Nothing draws men into the holy presence of God more completely than when they truly worship Him.

Worship is not the adulation or applause of some distant deity who cannot be approached by its subjects.

True worship is the heart…soul…mind and spirit drawing

in rich, warm fellowship. It is recognizing

itness, beauty and faithfulness, but most of

ous love He has for His children.

ship of Jehovah, the God of Heaven, is not killing anyone who does not accept your particular beliefs, as is the case of many overly zealous religions. Rather, it is offering God your affection, loyalty, aspiration and confidence.

When we realize that He bridged the gap between Himself and man, so that man could know the immenseness of His might and grace, worship will flow freely from the heart.

Worship is what God longs for from His children!

Jesus said:

God is a Spirit: and they that worship him must worship him in spirit and in truth.

JOHN 4:24

Anyone seeking God for a miracle touch, financial blessings or for personal direction will discover that "Worship," is a "Powerful Point of Contact!"

By now you realize the story line for this chapter comes from the Scriptural account of the Samaritan Woman meeting Jesus at Jacob's well.

When she met the Lord her life was a shambles, marriage vows, as far as she was concerned, were made only to be broken. Promiscuity was as normal for her as making the daily trip to the well for water. The future was no brighter than the past and religion was a duty rather than a joy.

She had tried to find inner peace by worshiping the way her fore-fathers worshiped, but for her the emptiness remained. She had religion, but it was void of life and there was no fulfillment in the ritualistic ceremonies.

I understand when men and women tell me they are disillusioned with religion. For many it is an effort in futility.

That's because people substitute religion for a genuine experience with God.

When I titled this chapter "He Really is A Know-it-All," I was thinking of the Samaritan woman's testimony to the people in her town.

The Bible says:

The woman then left her waterpot, and went her way into the city, and saith to the men, Come, see a man which told me all things that ever I did; is not this the Christ?

JOHN 4:29-30

Saying that someone is a "know-it-all" can, in most cases, be considered a derogatory statement, but when I say it about the Lord I mean it in the most congratulatory manner.

In effect I am saying, you never take him by surprise! God knows everything there is to know about you. He knows your weaknesses and your strengths. He knows the good and the bad in each of us and still He loves us.

The Samaritan woman was considered by the townspeople to be a tramp, a prostitute, a floozy, a no good from the wrong side of town. But what she was and the things she had done had no effect on Christ's love for her. When He arrived on the scene her life changed.

He has the wonderful ability to speak to a harlot and make her feel like a lady!

The story of the Samaritan woman is only one of hundreds of instances that prove conclusively that God knows the end from the beginning and everything in between.

Let me call your attention to four separate occasions at the beginning of Christ's earthly ministry that give credence to the statement that He, "Really is a Know-It-All."

Andrew was a follower of John the Baptist until he heard John say, *"Behold the Lamb of God!"* John was speaking about Jesus. From that moment, Andrew followed the Lord and became one of His most devoted disciples.

The first person Andrew witnessed to was his brother Simon. His statement to him was: *"We have found the Messiah!"*

And he brought him to Jesus.

Please note Jesus' first words to the great fisherman:

Thou art Simon the son of Jona; thou shalt be called Cephas, which is by interpretation, A stone.

JOHN 1:42 KJV

It is obvious that the Lord knew something about Cephas that no one else knew, because up to then and even after his initial meeting, the man was anything but a rock.

In fact it was not until the day of Pentecost when Cephas received the infilling of the Holy Spirit that Simon Peter began to fulfill his destiny as a rock solid preacher for Christ.

The second occasion that proved He is a "Know-It-All," was only a couple of days after He spoke prophetically to Peter.

This is how it happened:

As Jesus was leaving Galilee He found Philip and said, *"Follow me."*

Then Phillip found Nathanael and said to him, *"We have found him, of whom Moses in the law and the prophets did write, Jesus of Nazareth, the son of Joseph."*

When Nathanael heard that Jesus was from Nazareth he was not at all impressed. His only response was: *"Can there any good thing come out of Nazareth?"*

Philip had a great answer, *"Come and see."*

Jesus saw Nathanael coming to him, and saith unto him, Behold an Israelite indeed, in whom is no guile! Nathanael saith unto him, Whence knowest thou me? Jesus answered and said unto him, Before that Philip called thee, when thou wast under the fig tree, I saw thee.

JOHN 1:47-48 KJV

Something happened beneath the fig tree because when Jesus mentioned it to Nathanael he exclaimed: *"Rabbi, thou art the Son of God; thou art the King of Israel."*

While we don't know what took place under the tree, we do know that it became a "Powerful Point of Contact," for personal direction in Nathanael's life.

The third occasion happened in two parts. The first incident was just after Jesus began to minister to the people.

He and His disciples went to Jerusalem for the Passover feast. In the temple He found them selling oxen, sheep and doves, as well as money changers.

So, He made a scourge of small cords and drove them all out of the temple, including the sheep and oxen and He poured out the changers' money and overthrew the tables.

This outburst didn't set well with the Jews. They said to Him, *"What sign shewest thou unto us, seeing that thou doest these things? Jesus answered and said unto them, "Destroy this temple, and in three days I will raise it up."*

Jesus was showing the disciples that He knew He was going to die. When He said, *"Destroy this temple, and in three days I will raise it up."* He was referring to His body not the temple made of wood and stones.

When Jesus was raised from the dead the second part was fulfilled. His prediction and its fulfillment made such an impact on the disciples that the Bible said:

> ... *His disciples remembered that he had said this unto them; and they believed the scripture and the word which Jesus had said.*
>
> JOHN 2:22

Knowing that He knew the end from the beginning helped them to establish a "Powerful Point of Contact" for personal direction. They knew they could trust His word to be fulfilled.

The fourth occasion that proved conclusively that He "Really is A Know-It-All," is tucked away in three short verses.

While He was still in Jerusalem for the Passover feast, the Word says,

> ...*many believed in his name, when they saw the miracles which he did. But Jesus did not commit himself unto them, because he knew all men, And needed not that any should testify of man: for he knew what was in man.*
>
> John 2:23-25

Read that last verse again: *"And needed not that any should testify of man: for he knew what was in man."*

Let me repeat it one more time, and please remember, I'm not speaking disparagingly when I say, He "Really is A Know-It-All!" Rather, I am paying Him the highest compliment!

Knowing that He knows everything is a comfort to my soul. The future is not a worry to me! I refuse to be filled with fear and consternation... this world is His and He has it all under His divine control.

The Psalmist said:

> *The earth is the LORD'S, and the fullness thereof; the world, and they that dwell therein.*
>
> PSALM 24:1

God said of Himself:

**"*Who is like me, declaring the
end from the beginning?*"**

Yesterday is history, tomorrow a distant mystery; So I
have resolved that today, while it is day,
I will serve the Lord!

The Samaritan Woman, Simon Peter, Nathanael and the
other disciples established a "Powerful Point of Contact" for
personal direction by trusting in the knowledge of the Lord.

You can establish your very own, "Powerful Point of
Contact" when you recognize that with Him there are no
surprises! He who knows everything is aware of where you
are and what you need today!

Seize this opportunity to receive your miracle through
worship, prayer and praise!

Section Two

Conclusion

In the final analysis it should be clear to everyone that God desires a personal relationship with His children. He is always ready to reveal Himself to the hungry in spirit.

You can be the beneficiary of these great promises if you act on the Word:

> *Draw nigh to God, and he will draw nigh to you. Cleanse your hands, ye sinners; and purify your hearts, ye double minded. Be afflicted, and mourn, and weep: let your laughter be turned to mourning, and your joy to heaviness. Humble yourselves in the sight of the Lord, and he shall lift you up.*
>
> JAMES 4:8-10

Remember...King David did not rely on yesterday's direction when he fought against the Philistines. He sought the mind of God for each new battle plan. You and I need to do the same when we encounter the devil.

God will order your footsteps as you seek Him for your "Powerful Point of Contact" for personal direction!

Section Three

Introduction

Financial independence will forever be a far-fetched dream in the minds of many people! Not because it's God's will, but because they will never do what it takes to break the poverty syndrome and move into His wonderful land of plenty.

Establishing your very own, "Powerful Point of Contact" for Prosperity, as you will discover in this section, is not difficult, but it does require participation on your part.

One of the greatest truths you will learn in these chapters is that no one has to become poor for you to become rich.

When God created the heavens and the earth He deposited enough wealth in the earth to make all of his children rich...rich...rich beyond their wildest dreams.

Heaven, with its streets of gold, walls of jasper and gates of pearl, is more opulent than mortal man can ever imagine.

Does the God who lives in such a place of glory and splendor expect His sons and daughters to live in poverty, squalor and want?

You'll find the answer to this and many other probing questions in this very important section.

Prosperity will never be a reality for those who live with a poverty mentality! On these pages you will discover the great truths of the Word that can help you break the bondages of the devil and help you move into God's world of plenty!

Section Three

Chapter 10
Counting The Apples In A Seed

Any fool can count the seeds in an apple...but God can count the apples in a seed. Let me share a story that I heard many years ago!

An eminent servant was given the privilege of making the arrangements for the king's twenty-fifth anniversary celebration.

Although the glorious event was still more than five years away, even the smallest detail was carefully planned, the servant made certain that everything was perfect for the king whom he loved.

When planning the menu he wanted to present the king and his guests with extraordinary baked goods so he took a special strain of wheat which had been passed down in his family for many generations.

Holding a single grain in his hand he said, "I am giving you the responsibility of providing loaves of bread, delicate rolls and delicious sweets for the king's banquet!"

"But," the little grain of wheat protested, "I'm so small, how can I do it all alone?"

The servant spoke with the wisdom of an angel as he said to the grain of wheat, "I will place you in good soil and gently cover you, at first it will be dark and cold and you will think you are going to die, but don't be afraid.

It is only by placing you in good soil that you experience growth. Then you will reproduce and feed the guests at the king's grand banquet. It is only when you are planted that you experience the miracle of multiplication.

Jesus said it this way:

> *I assure you, most solemnly I tell you, Unless a grain of wheat falls into the earth and dies, it remains [just one grain; never becomes more but lives] by itself alone. But if it dies, it produces many others and yields a rich harvest.*
>
> JOHN 12:24 AMP

So the wise servant placed the little grain in the ground and sure enough it multiplied, so he planted each new grain and they multiplied. Again and again he planted each seed until fields were waving with golden grains of wheat and the king's guests were all fed from one single seed.

Never underestimate the potential of a single seed planted in good soil!

This section of the book is dedicated to helping you establish a "Powerful Point of Contact," for releasing God's abundant financial blessings in your life.

Nothing you ever do will prove to be more effective financially than planting in good soul-winning soil.

I can't count the times I've had people say to me, "Brother Cerullo, for years I've been faithful with my tithes and offerings, but I've never had a financial breakthrough. Why doesn't God bless and prosper me like I hear of Him doing for other people?"

My answer is always the same, "Have you checked the soil you're planting in?"

I have met many Christians who treat giving as if it were a spiritual lottery. They run here and there, giving a few dollars to one ministry after another hoping that some day they will have the **lucky** prayer prayed over them and they will strike it rich.

Sadly, hundreds of other good people honestly believe if they go to church and give in the offerings God will be pleased with them and they will be automatically blessed. Then they come to me in tears, because they continue to struggle through life barely making ends meet.

They never stop to realize that nothing is automatic, you have to make it happen.

Each of these groups are chasing the wind! When I hear their lamented stories I want to say again, "Have you checked the soil you're planting in?"

Simply believing that if you give to the church or that you give to a particular ministry will result in a blessing is as ludicrous as believing you will reap a bumper crop if you plant apples in the Sahara Desert and oranges in Anchorage Alaska.

You can plant ten thousand Washington State Delicious apple seeds in the middle of the desert and a truck-load of sweet, juicy Navel orange seeds in a snow bank in Alaska, if you choose.

Common sense, however, will tell you that you have wasted good seed and you will not reap a harvest. Why? Because the soil and the climate in those areas are not suited for those particular seeds!

Keep in mind the marvelous revelation that I have taught you, that all truth is parallel. If it makes sense to plant in the right soil to grow apples and oranges it is equally true in the spiritual. If you want God's bountiful blessings to flow in ever increasing abundance, then you must plant in soul-winning soil.

If you are angry or disappointed with God for not blessing you for your giving let me ask you, "How long it has been since you saw a sinner weeping in repentance at the church altar? Or, do you even have an altar in the church any longer?"

"When was the last time your pastor preached a message that tugged at the heartstrings of sinners and or made the hypocrite squirm in the pew?" "Is your church a museum for saints or a hospital for sinners?"

I promise you, God is looking for churches and ministries that are more interested in winning the lost than in building large structures.

Am I against beautiful churches? No! A thousand times, NO! How could I, a Jew, object to building a majestic house for God? My people, ancient Israel had one of the most magnificent temples ever constructed anywhere.

The stones of that glorious temple were all cut and numbered in the quarry so that each one fit exactly. The ceiling was made from the fabled cedars of Lebanon and overlaid with gold and the curtain that divided the sanctuary from the holy of holies was so thick that twelve yoke of oxen pulling in opposite directions could not tear it.

I am not against building something outstanding for God, but if all the efforts are to build an edifice for pomp and show and to be the most elegant place in town, it is a church without a vision. And if that is where you are investing your money then you might as well be planting apple seeds in the middle of the desert!

It's much easier to find God in a store-front church that is reaching out to win souls than in a cathedral where there is no passion for the lost.

I've been asked many times why World Evangelism partners are so blessed and prosperous. The answer should be obvious to everyone. It's because the core of this ministry shares the heartbeat of God...souls...souls...souls!

If you are not experiencing the full rich blessings of God in your life, if you are not walking in divine health, and being prospered on a daily basis then hear the admonition of God's prophet, **check the soil you are planting in.**

Let me repeat something I said earlier in this chapter:

Never underestimate the potential of a single seed planted in good soil!

Once when I was in the mountains, walking among a stand of beautiful oak trees, my attention was called to a single acorn laying on the ground. I heard a voice say, pick it up. I obeyed and stood quietly holding it in my hand, waiting for the voice to continue speaking. I'll never forget the lesson I learned that day.

The voice said, "The little acorn you hold in your hand has the full potential of being a hundred, a thousand or even tens of thousands of oak trees. Resident in that one small acorn is everything it takes to be a mighty forest."

I realized that as long as I held it in my hand, it would never be anything but an acorn. It would never grow, rather, it would wither, the life inside it would vanish and its potential would be lost.

I could lay it on a rock for a bird or a squirrel or some other wild animal to eat or I could take it from its mountain home and cast it out along the highway where it would be crushed.

Or...I could plant it with my blessing and believe that it would be nourished by sun and rain and by virtue of that which God had placed within, it would become the majestic oak it was destined to be.

If I could be there with you right now I would slice an apple in half so you and I could remove the seeds and count them, then I would ask you to take one of the seeds in your hand, close your eyes and imagine how many thousands of apple trees that one little seed could produce. I'm certain you would say to me, "There is no end to what one seed can generate!"

It is absolutely mind boggling to think of the vast potential one little seed has when it is planted in good soil.

Jesus gave us this illustration:

...Behold, the sower went out to sow; and as he sowed, some seeds fell beside the road, and the birds came and ate them up. And others fell on the rocky places, where they did not have much soil; and immediately they sprang up, because they had no depth of soil. But when the sun was risen, they were scorched; and because they had no root, they withered away. Others fell among the thorns, and the thorns came up and choked them out. And others fell on the good soil, and yielded a crop, some a hundredfold, some sixty, and some thirty. He who has ears, let him hear.

MATTHEW 13:3-9 NAS

Let me go back to my last statement prior to the Words of Jesus...

It is absolutely mind boggling to think of the vast potential one little seed has when it is planted in good soil.

The famous wine country of Northern California is a prime example of what one seed planted in good soil can do. Many of the vineyards in that area were planted by immigrants from Italy, Germany and France, three of the principle wine producing countries of Europe.

When the people set out from their homelands to start a new life in America, they carefully packed some seedlings from the vineyards back home and brought them with them to this country and searched for the proper soil and climate so they could be planted.

The results have been phenomenal! Thanks to those enterprising men and women the vineyards in America are producing some of the finest grapes in the world. And can you imagine that it all started with one small seed.

The stories of seeds to success are so numerous it is impossible to tell all of them.

Farmers in America have transformed the windswept plains into fertile fields, trees have been planted and forests have grown up all around us to furnish the materials for building homes across this great land. The flowers that decorate our houses and lawns and dot the landscape from sea to shining sea, each come from a little seed.

Never underestimate the potential
of a single seed planted in good soil!

You have heard me say many times, "Give your seed a name." I tell you that because when you name your seed, you can also name your need.

Throughout this chapter I have talked to you about establishing a "Powerful Point of Contact," for releasing God's financial blessings in your life and the necessity of planting the seed, which more than likely is money. God has placed a certain amount of money at your disposal to be used as seed.

It is crucial that you recognize this vital truth...your seed will not reproduce as long as you hold it in your hand. It will not reproduce in the bank, or in the stock market. Oh, it will draw a little interest or if you place it in stocks and bonds it may possibly yield a small return, but if you are thinking in terms of a harvest then you must plant in the fertile soil of world evangelism.

God does not promise to bless monies put in the bank for

safe keeping, but He has promised thirty, sixty and one hundred fold return for seed invested in His Kingdom.

My greatest desire is to arm you with a plan that will bless and keep on blessing you from this day forward. I am not espousing a get-rich-quick scheme, rather, a lifestyle that you can live with and continue to walk in God's abundance.

Too many people treat prosperity like a weight loss program where they do a crash diet for a few days to get ready for a wedding, or a beach vacation, where they look good for an occasion.

God's plan of prosperity for your life is not simply to provide a new car or a dress or suit for a special party. He wants you to experience life to the fullest. He is concerned with today, tomorrow and all your tomorrow's.

In each story in this chapter I have talked about planting a seed. Whether it was the single grain of wheat that was given the responsibility for providing bread and rolls for the king's banquet, the little acorn in the mountains or the beautiful vineyards in the fertile California, Napa Valley, one principle remained consistent, every seed must be planted and a portion of that which is produced must be re-planted.

For anyone to enjoy the bounties of a perpetual harvest they must be willing to plant and plant and plant! You cannot possibly plant one time and reap for a lifetime. A perpetual harvest is dependent on perpetual planting.

Prosperity is not an illusive dream!

Prosperity is not the luck of the draw and it is not an illusive dream. It is a dynamic promise from the Father to His obedient children. Your prosperity or the lack thereof, is dependent entirely on your response to God.

Look at the opening statement of this chapter again,

"Any fool can count the seeds in an apple, but God can count the apples in a seed!"

God does not need your money to keep His vast universe operating smoothly, but you need His blessings to keep the wheels of your vehicle called life from falling off.

Once you truly understand this glorious truth you will never have another problem obeying when the Holy Spirit tells you to give. God never speaks to you to give without first planning an abundant harvest especially for you.

STOP!

READ THAT STATEMENT ONE MORE TIME!

God never speaks to you to give without first planning an abundant harvest especially for you!

In his second letter to the Corinthian Church Paul wrote these words of encouragement:

[Remember] this he who sows sparingly and grudgingly will also reap sparingly and grudgingly, and he who sows generously [that blessings may come to someone], will also reap generously and with blessings. Let each of one [give] as he has made up his own mind and purposed in his heart, not reluctantly or sorrowfully or under compulsion, for God loves (that is, He takes pleasure in, prizes above other things, and is unwilling to abandon or to do without) a cheerful (joyous, prompt-to-do-it) giver [whose heart is in his giving]. And God is able to make all grace (every favor and earthly blessing) come to you in abundance, so that you may always and under all circumstances and whatever the need, be self-sufficient [possessing enough to require no aid or support and furnished in abundance for every good work and charitable donation].

II Corinthians 9: 6-8 AMP

God is not in the poverty business! He is not the one who makes people poor, penniless and destitute. Those are part of the curse that came upon mankind in the Garden of Eden.

As a child of God you have divine rights and privileges and one of those rights is "choice!" The moment you accepted Christ as your Savior, He placed inside your heart the ability to choose the path you will walk and the voice you will obey.

You don't have to be broke and on the brink of disaster.

You don't have to wear hand-me-downs and eat left-overs, drive a beat up old wreck or live in a cardboard shack. You are a member of the Royal Family of Heaven.

This is what the Bible says:

> *And [God] Who provides seed for the sower and bread for eating will also provide and multiply your [resources for] sowing, and increase the fruits of your righteousness [which manifests itself in active goodness, kindness and charity].*
>
> II CORINTHIANS 9:10

Make up your mind that you are a "sower!" Your "Powerful Point of Contact" for releasing God's financial blessings in your life is summed up in the words of Christ.

He said:

> *Give, and it shall be given unto you; good measure, pressed down, and shaken together, and running over, shall men give into your bosom. For with the same measure that ye mete withal it shall be measured to you again.*
>
> LUKE 6:38

Any fool can count the seeds in an apple, but God can

count the apples in a seed.

Do you realize that God put enough apples in every seed to feed a hungry world, but more often than not they are carelessly cast aside?

Your "Powerful Point of Contact" for releasing God's financial blessings is in planting the seed He has placed in your hand. Plant it and when it produces a harvest, plant a portion of the harvest. Give and keep on giving and you will be on your way to reaping the perpetual harvest God promised in His Word.

Section Three

Chapter 11

Gathering Sticks
And Moving Up

There was precious little for the widow to hope for. Her husband was dead, a terrible drought had reduced the beautiful farmland to stubble and her cupboard was bare.

She had just enough oil and meal to make a little cake for her son and herself. After that one meager dinner was finished she would wash the dishes, clean the house and wait for death to claim its victims.

How long she and her son could survive was a question she didn't want to consider. All too soon she would see a hollow look in his eyes, then the swollen belly and finally the terrible rattle of death in his breathing.

Death, by starvation is a horrible thing to witness, but it's even worse when it's you own child you are watching die!

We have no idea how long the little widow had put off making their last meal...a day...three days...a week? She knew that when she prepared that last little cake, death was not far away.

Finally, the fateful day arrived, so she went out to gather a few sticks to build a fire and cook their last meal. Little did she know that she was going to be given a Rhema, a divine word from God that would change her life forever.

As the widow started her death march in search of sticks, Elijah, the prophet of God was on a life march in search of a widow who would hear and obey his words.

Let's tune in to the conversation:

"Then the word of the LORD came to him, saying,

Arise, go to Zarephath, which belongs to Sidon, and stay there; behold, I have commanded a widow there to provide for you. So he arose and went to Zarephath, and when he came to the gate of the city, behold, a widow was there gathering sticks; and he called to her and said, Please get me a little water in a jar, that I may drink. As she was going to get it, he called to her and said, Please bring me a piece of bread in your hand. But she said, As the LORD your God lives, I have no bread, only a handful of flour in the bowl and a little oil in the jar; and behold, I am gathering a few sticks that I may go in and prepare for me and my son, that we may eat it and die. Then Elijah said to her, Do not fear; go, do as you have said, but make me a little bread cake from it first and bring it out to me, and afterward you may make one for yourself and for your son. For thus says the LORD God of Israel, The bowl of flour shall not be exhausted, nor shall the jar of oil be empty, until the day that the LORD sends rain on the face of the earth. So she went and did according to the word of Elijah, and she and he and her household ate for many days. The bowl of flour was not exhausted nor did the jar of oil become empty, according to the word of the LORD which He spoke through Elijah.

1 KINGS 17:8-16 NAS

The widow of Zarephath was a chosen vessel of the Lord. The fact that she didn't know what God was doing had no bearing on the blessing He was preparing for her.

Through obedience she was going to discover her "Powerful Point of Contact." She was on the verge of a miracle when she thought she was doomed to die.

I want you to catch a glimpse of the magnitude of God's miracle in this woman's life, keeping in mind that the miracle would have never materialized had she not been obedient to the word of the prophet. His word was her "Powerful Point of Contact."

What a paradox, the widow was resigned not only to die, but to watching her son die as well. But... her resignation to a slow painful death was not at all what God had in mind for her.

Here's the blockbuster truth, even though she thought she was on the brink of disaster, through obedience to the man of God, she turned tragedy into triumph.

I'm always amazed with the way God does things. Like a pastor friend of mine says, "God is never late but He misses some wonderful opportunities to be early."

You may be asking, "Why did the Lord wait until the widow's meal barrel was virtually empty and the oil cruse was almost dry before He came to her rescue?"

I'll tell you why!

God works miracles when all else fails. He does it this way, because He wants you and me to know that wonders are performed for His people and that we are to give Him all the glory. Men are not miracle workers!

God orchestrates things too big, too awesome and too grand for the finite mind of man. Notice the series of events He brought to pass in order to work the miracle for the widow.

First, He caused the brook where Elijah was hanging out to go dry. This necessitated a change in the prophet's plans. That's when God told him to go to Zarephath.

Next, He told the prophet that He had commanded a widow to provide for him. He didn't bother to tell Elijah that a second meal at her house would take a miracle. Nor did God tell him that He had made no mention of any of this to the widow. In other words... she wasn't expecting company!

You may be wondering why God said He had commanded the widow to provide for the prophet without mentioning it to the woman. That's because God looks on the heart and through His infinite wisdom He knew the widow would obey.

Is the same true about you? If your circumstances were as bleak and daunting as hers would you share your last meal with the prophet of God?

Before you answer that question think back to the last time the Lord spoke to you to give... did you obey? Did you obey quickly or did you question the authenticity of His voice?

If your needs are staggering and you don't know where the money is coming from to pay your bills... do you quickly answer yes, when the prophet asks you to sacrifice?

When you look at the widows circumstances through the eyes of your own needs you understand what a great sacrifice she made to the Lord. It's no wonder that her story made it into the Word of God.

Then God brought the widow and the prophet together by divine appointment. Oh, she didn't realize that she was walking into a miracle when she left her house that day. The widow simply thought that she was going out to pick up a few sticks so she could build a fire and cook her last meal.

Divine appointments have always intrigued me. I remember my first one. I had left the Daughters of Miriam

Orphanage, because I couldn't stand one more beating from the Rabbi to make me deny my new-found faith in my Messiah.

The night was bitter cold. A blizzard had struck New Jersey in full fury and I was out on the street without a coat. I left the orphanage in such a rush that I didn't even get my jacket.

Scarcely had I stepped out on the street than I realized I didn't have my coat or any money. I hadn't eaten and didn't know where I was going. The one thing I did know... I could never, never, never go back to the orphanage!

The gale-force wind and snow pelted my face when I lifted my eyes heavenward and asked God to please help me find my way.

I will never forget the warmth of His presence as He walked up beside me, took me by the hand and led me to the very spot that I was to meet Mrs. Ethel Kerr. Mrs. Kerr is the lady who first told me about Christ.

That was my first divine appointment. Since that time there have been many more. One in particular was six months prior to the Six Day War in the Middle East. God said to me, "Son it's time to turn your face to My people Israel!"

That divine appointment completely changed my ministry and has, in many ways, changed the face of Israel. From the time the Holy Spirit spoke to me we have flooded the land with the Gospel of the risen Messiah through the printed page, healing rallies and television.

God doesn't make divine appointments just to make people feel religious or to produce warm fuzzies. He makes divine appointments so men and women can establish a "Powerful Point of Contact!"

Remember, God is a God of design, purpose, objective and plan! He doesn't do things just to be doing. When God directs your path He has a divine purpose in mind. And...

when He speaks to you to give, He has a bountiful harvest planned especially for you.

No sooner had the widow started to pick up sticks than Elijah the prophet came to the gate of the city and called to her, *"Please get me a little water in a jar, that I may drink."*

Don't underestimate the prophet's first request, remember there was a drought throughout the land and water was a precious commodity. In fact, water was one of the most precious things anyone had.

When the prophet asked for a drink he was asking the widow to make a sacrifice and give the servant of God that which was precious to her.

As I write this book, the American farmers across the plains states and the Western United States are suffering from a drought. Rainfall has been so sparse in the West that in many major cities people can be fined for watering their lawns.

Imagine what it would be like if not one drop of rain fell on America for two, two-and-a-half or three years!

That's what it was like in Israel when Elijah arrived in Zarephath and the drought was not over. So when he asked for a little water he was requesting something that was precious to her.

But…he didn't stop there! *"As she was going to get it, he called to her and said, "Please bring me a piece of bread in your hand."* Remember, God told the prophet that He had commanded the widow to provide for him so his request was valid.

Up to this point Elijah had no inclination of her dire circumstances. All he knew was that he had a need and that God told him this little widow was His chosen vessel.

But she said,

> *As the LORD your God lives, I have no bread, only a*

*handful of flour in the bowl and a little oil in the jar;
and behold, I am gathering a few sticks that I may go in
and prepare for me and my son, that we may eat it and
die.*

Had Elijah been a man of weak faith, the widow's
confession could have caused him to reconsider his options
and to doubt that her address was the right one.

What thoughts would run through your mind if you were
to take up residence in a home where the cupboard was
empty and the occupants were resigned to starving to death?

Thank God Elijah was not moved by what he saw or heard
from the woman. The widow's circumstances necessitated a
miracle. Isn't it wonderful that miracles are a specialty with God?

Keep this vital truth in mind; if you want the Lord to do
the supernatural, it is imperative that you do your part.

The prophet's next statement challenged the widow to
look beyond the impossible, beyond the bigness of her need
to the bigness of the God of Israel!

*Then Elijah said to her, Do not fear; go, do as you
have said, but make me a little bread cake from it first
and bring it out to me, and afterward you may make
one for yourself and for your son. For thus says the
LORD God of Israel, The bowl of flour shall not be
exhausted, nor shall the jar of oil be empty, until the
day that the LORD sends rain on the face of the earth.*

Can you imagine what would happen today if a preacher
asked a poor, indigent, threadbare widow to share her last
morsel of food with him?

The news media would have a field-day! His picture
would be splashed across the front page of every leading
newspaper in the land. Television cameras would follow him
wherever he went and the goody-goody commentators would

brand him as a charlatan, a cheat and a disgrace to society.

Can't you just hear the evening news anchor repeat the prophet's words with a sneer in his voice?

Do not fear; go, do as you have said, but make me a little bread cake from it first and bring it out to me, and afterward you may make one for yourself and for your son.

Oh yes! "Make me a little bread cake first and bring it out to me!" Never mind that there isn't enough for the poor widow or her son, just so the preacher gets his first!

Praise God, the widow didn't wait for the evening news to pick up on her sad plight. Rather, she established a "Powerful Point of Contact" to release her faith and receive her miracle!

The Bible declares:

So she went and did according to the word of Elijah, and she and he and her household ate for many days. The bowl of flour was not exhausted nor did the jar of oil become empty, according to the word of the LORD which He spoke through Elijah.

This is the part of the story that thrills me the most!

I don't know if you have ever paid close attention to what the Word says, *"So she went and did according to the word of Elijah,* **and she and he and her household ate for many days."**

Wait...wait...wait! Throughout this entire story the only people mentioned were Elijah, the widow and her son! So why the mention of her household all of a sudden? Who is this household and how did they get into the picture?

I'll tell you!

When the widow was in need and on the verge of

starvation her family avoided her like the plague. In all likelihood, they were in the same predicament and couldn't have offered help even if they wanted to. But when the blessing of God flooded her life there was plenty for her, the prophet, her son and her household.

I remember hearing a sermon on this portion of Scripture several years ago. The minister went into great detail of how each time the little widow started to make another cake for herself and her son it was always the last bit of flour and the last few drops of oil in the cruse.

I recall thinking, "Why wouldn't God just go ahead and fill the flour barrel and the oil vessel rather than measuring a little at a time?" Why would He keep everyone on poverty row not knowing from one day to the next if there would be another meal?

That's when the Lord gave me a "Rhema," a supernatural word from Heaven. He spoke to me to read a particular passage in Luke's Gospel.

Let me share it with you!

Give, and it will be given to you; they will pour into your lap a good measure, pressed down, shaken together, running over, . For by your standard of measure it will be measured to you in return.

LUKE 6:38 NAS

I want you to pay close attention to the punctuation of this verse. Notice the comma after the word "Give," it's there because when you give you set the wheels of prosperity into motion.

Jesus said, *"Give, and it will be given to you!"* What did Jesus say would be given to you? "IT!" What did He mean? Whatever you give! That's the "IT" that will be given to you.

The widow gave flour and oil. That's why the Bible said the flour barrel didn't go empty and the oil cruse didn't go dry.

But there is more to Luke 6:38, let's read the rest of the verse. *"It will be given to you; they will pour into your lap a good measure, pressed down, shaken together, running over, For by your standard of measure it will be measured to you in return."*

How did Jesus say it will be given to you? *"They will pour into your lap, a good measure, pressed down, shaken together, running over."*

Partner, that's exactly what I see happening to the little widow I've been writing about. I don't believe she had to struggle every day, barely having enough to keep soul and body together.

I believe God stepped across the pages of the future, took the promise of His Son and planted it in the life of that faithful woman. When she returned from delivering the little cake to the man of God, she found her flour barrel heaped up and the oil cruse full to the brim.

The widow of Zarephath had established a "Powerful Point of Contact" for receiving her miracle of supply. Her "Powerful Point of Contact" was obedience to the word of the man of God.

It is interesting to note that there is no mention of her talking to God. When the prophet spoke she didn't put out a "fleece" to see if it was really God. She didn't call in a committee and take a vote and she didn't ask someone's advice. She simply obeyed! She was ready to quit gathering sticks and move up!

I can't tell you how many times the Lord has challenged men and women to give through his prophet. When they obey, the miracles begin to happen. I have seen it happen throughout the length and breadth of the earth.

Here is the secret that will set you free! It wasn't Elijah

who created the miracle of abundance for the widow, and it isn't Morris Cerullo who has created financial miracles for thousands of people all over the world. It is obedience to the man of God that creates the miracle of abundance.

The moment you hear God's prophet challenge you to do something special for His Kingdom, if you will obey, your obedience will become your "Powerful Point of Contact" for financial freedom.

Elijah didn't ask the widow for her last cake to speed up the starvation process. He didn't ask her to give, because he was selfish and didn't care about her needs. He asked her to give so "IT" could be given to her, good measure, pressed down, shaken together and running over!

Every time God challenges you to give He has a harvest planned especially for you!

Circle the word **Obedience**, it's your
"Powerful Point of Contact," for abundant living!

Don't wait another day... purpose in your heart that you are going to change your destiny by acting in obedience to the voice of the Lord when He speaks through His prophet.

Section Three

Chapter 12
Divine Retirement

Bitterness toward God could have filled the woman's heart, after all, she and her husband had been faithful to work for God; in fact, her husband was a minister.

In Old Testament times the ministry was made up of two main divisions, the priesthood which came from the tribe of Levi and the sons of the prophets.

The chief priests descended from the house of Aaron and had the responsibility of offering sacrifices and making atonement for the people.

The sons of the prophets were men who received a divine call from God and were generally the ones who called Israel and Judah to repentance.

These sons of the prophets were a special group who studied at the feet of the prophets. They were also in a separate category from the priesthood in that they derived their livelihood from the generosity of the people.

A portion of the tithe the people brought to God went to the priests, but the sons of the prophets were not entitled to share in the tithe, so they had to depend on God and the generosity of the people for their sustenance.

In the days of Elijah and Elisha, two of the greatest prophets in the long, illustrious history of Israel and Judah the sons of the prophets played an important roll in keeping the message of God before the people.

The lady featured in this chapter was married to one of the sons of the prophets who met an untimely death that left her in a destitute condition.

Let's pick up on her conversation with the Prophet Elisha!

A certain woman of the wives of the sons of the prophets cried out to Elisha, saying, "Your servant my husband is dead, and you know that your servant feared the LORD. And the creditor is coming to take my two sons to be his slaves.

Before I go any farther with this chapter I want to impress on your heart a very important truth. God does not intend for His children to live a life of indebtedness.

It is God's will for you to be debt free!

In this chapter you will discover the secret to establishing a "Powerful Point of Contact" that will help you receive your miracle of **debt free living.**

If this sounds too good to be true... then just keep reading, there is a miracle awaiting you!

The widow who came to the prophet was faced with the grim prospect of losing her two sons to slavery because she didn't have enough money to pay the debts she and her husband had incurred. This was after seeing her husband go to an untimely grave.

Since this book is dedicated to helping you establish a "Powerful Point of Contact" for touching God and receiving a miracle in your life I won't go into great discussion about controlling your spending urges.

I will remind you, however, that God expects His children to use prudence with their finances. You cannot consistently spend more than you earn and not get into a financial trap.

As you read the story of this woman keep in mind that neither you, nor I, nor anyone else has a lease on life. Any day of the week we could be called to be with the Lord, so it is incumbent upon us to always live within our means.

Somehow, the woman who came to Elisha and her husband had never heard that part of the sermon. They got caught up in the buy now...pay later falsehood, so when He died the wife was left with all the unpaid bills.

Not knowing where else to go she came to the man of God with her heart-wrenching story.

So Elisha said to her, What shall I do for you? Tell me, what do you have in the house? And she said, Your maidservant has nothing in the house but a jar of oil.

Do you remember the lesson I taught you earlier about the difference between fact and truth? The answer the woman gave Elisha was not truth. The fact was she had nothing but a jar of oil. The truth was entirely different; that jar of oil was attached to something she had never seen.

It is extremely important to remember that when you need a miracle the first step is to recognize what you have rather than what you want. Your miracle is never far away when you see the bigness of God and not the bigness of your need.

Elisha helped her to establish a "Powerful Point of Contact," so she could release her faith for a great miracle.

Notice what the man of God told her to do:

Go, borrow vessels from everywhere, from all your neighbors – empty vessels; do not gather just a few. And when you have come in, you shall shut the door behind you and your sons;

The thought of borrowing anything probably sent cold shivers running up her spine. After all, that's what got her in trouble in the first place. Now the prophet was telling her to go deeper in debt.

Don't always expect the man of God to tell you what you want to hear!

There are several things about this story that just do not make sense in the natural. For one thing, when you are over your head in debt, it isn't good to keep on borrowing.

Reason and common sense will tell you that you can't borrow your way out of debt! But God is not bound by common sense and reason.

Had the widow questioned the man of God he could have reminded her of the time God told Moses to have the children of Israel borrow silver, gold and jewels from their neighbors.

When they were ready to leave the land of Egypt, God used that method to repay them for the hundreds of years they had served as slaves.

Several times in my ministry I have heard God telling me to challenge individuals to give when it was impossible for them to obey without borrowing. I have never known of God failing to bless and restore, thirty, sixty or a hundred fold when they acted in obedience to the man of God!

There were six dramatic steps to the woman's deliverance. The first two things Elisha told her to do were, "borrow vessels and shut the door.

Now...why would the prophet tell her to shut the door when she went in her house? I'll tell you! The woman didn't need any outside interference.

God was going to do a wonderful work in her life and the last thing she needed was for someone to stand around telling her what to expect. The same is true for you! When you have heard from God, shut out the world and let Him work through you.

The third thing the prophet told her to do was pour!

pour it into all those vessels, and set aside the full ones. So she went from him and shut the door behind her and her sons, who brought the vessels to her; and she poured it out.

Elisha told her to "pour" today...so she wouldn't be "poor" tomorrow!

Can you imagine what went through that widow's mind when she went into her house, shut the door and looked at all the vessels they had borrowed?

All she had was one jar of oil and the prophet had told her to pour out of it into the vessels. As impossible as it looked in the natural, it was the best plan she had. In reality it was her only plan.

When she acted in faith and obeyed the prophet God drilled an oil-well in her kitchen!

When I read this story I can almost feel the excitement that charged the atmosphere when she started pouring from her one jar of oil and she could see the oil rising to the top of the first borrowed vessel. "Bring me another one," she called to her son and they both watched in wide-eyed wonderment as the oil rose up to the top of the second container, then the third and the fourth.

How could so much oil flow from one single jar? How could they fill big ones from a little one? What kind of magic had the prophet worked to make such a thing happen?

It wasn't magic and it wasn't an illusion, she was actually filling container after container from the one jar she had in her home. Because...

When she acted in faith and obeyed the prophet God

drilled an oil-well in her kitchen!

The oil this well produced was better than "Texas Crude" or Saudi "Black Gold!" God drilled a gusher in her kitchen and it was producing "Pure... Extra Virgin Olive Oil!"

The widow followed the prophet's advice to the letter and through it, established her very own, "Powerful Point of Contact" for a financial miracle. Obedience was her catalyst for a miracle, it was her, "Powerful Point of Contact!"

Now it came to pass, when the vessels were full, that she said to her son, Bring me another vessel. And he said to her, There is not another vessel. So the oil ceased.

I heard a preacher talking about how she missed a golden opportunity. He said that if she had known what God was going to do she would have had a fleet of tanker trucks sitting in her front yard and a cargo ship waiting in the bay.

The truth is God was at work the entire time! He knew exactly how many vessels she needed, so when she and her sons went out to borrow, He had already touched the hearts of the lenders and He had the oil measured before she began to pour.

This story reminds me of a man in South-eastern Oklahoma. The man was a fine Christian who really loved the Lord and didn't want anything to come between him and God.

When oil was discovered on farms all around his, he fell on his face before The Lord and prayed a prayer something like this, "Oh God, You know I love You and I don't want anything to hinder me from doing Your will. Now Lord, if finding oil on my land will fill my heart with worldly desires don't let there be any. And if there is, don't let it be more than I can handle and stay humble in Your sight."

The geologists had ascertained that the largest pool of oil

in the area was under this man's land and when they started to drill everyone expected to hit a "gusher!"

No one would have ever guessed that the wells on his land would be dribblers, but that's what happened.

Now you may think "What a wonderful answer to prayer," but the truth is the man was on the brink of a miracle and he allowed unbelief to shut off God's blessings.

The prayer that man should have prayed was, "Lord stretch me and enlarge my capacity, so I can be a blessing to the Kingdom of God." Imagine all the good he could have done for missions and world evangelism had he asked God to help him hit gushers, rather than dribblers.

Imagine all the souls that could have been reached in his lifetime had he set his sights on being a rich man for Christ and making God his partner rather than cowering in fear, believing that money would contaminate his heart.

God is looking for men and women He can trust with the riches of this world. He is searching the earth today for partners who will say to Him, "You can trust me to bless Your Kingdom and win the lost throughout the world."

I believe God is prepared to raise up some new "Bill Gates!" Get ready, because the ones He is raising up will finance the Gospel to the ends of the earth.

Will God expect this new generation of fabulously wealthy men and women to live like paupers while they spread the Word to the lost and dying? Absolutely not!

The rest of the widow's story will prove conclusively that God wants to bless and prosper His children! When He performs a financial miracle for us He does it for our comfort as well as for us to be able to reach out to the lost.

Do you recall me saying earlier that the prophet told her

six things to do? We have discussed the first three, "Borrow, Shut the door and Pour." There are three items left on the prophet's agenda!

Let's see what they are!

Then she came and told the man of God. And he said, Go, sell the oil and pay your debt.

The miracle of the oil flowing to fill the vessels was what God did, the remainder was up to the widow.

That's when the prophet told her:

Sell the oil!

I've often wondered how the widow marketed the oil. Did she tell her customers that it was miracle oil? That would have been a totally correct statement! No one could have sued her for false advertising. Not only had she witnessed the miracle, but her two sons were also eye witnesses.

Perhaps she simply asked her customers to smell the oil. It was certain that none of them had ever smelled a fresher product, even those who pressed their own olives. God had bypassed the whole process of growing, gathering and pressing by creating the finished product from the start.

Maybe she held it up to the light and let them see the pure clean product sparkle in the sun or poured a drop into the palm of the ladies hand so she could feel the luxurious lubrication of the miracle product.

Or she could have given the buyer a taste! I have to tell you, as a connoisseur of olive oil, nothing is more pleasing to the palate than fresh pressed olive oil. Wine is aged in barrels to produce its best flavor, but olive oil is best immediately after it is pressed.

You may be certain that the discerning buyer knows the difference between fresh olive oil and that which was processed last year. No one had ever tasted fresher oil than what the widow was selling.

Step number five...PAY your debt!

This is such an important step for every child of God to take note of. Too many people think the minute they get money in their hands they have to rush out and spend it.

God doesn't intend for His children to spend, spend, spend each time He blesses them, rather that their debts can be paid and they can live free of the debt trap. Another thing to remember is that He blesses us so that we can pay our vows to Him.

"Divine Retirement"

As you've read the story of the widow, who was about to lose her two sons as slaves to the creditor, you have no doubt asked yourself, what is there in this story that lends itself to "Divine Retirement?" Is there some relevance or is that just the title of the chapter?

You'll find the answer to that question in the sixth and final step Elisha gave to the widow. Don't forget, she discovered her "Powerful Point of Contact" for financial independence was **Obedience** to the man of God.

She had obeyed to the letter when Elisha said, "Borrow, Shut the door, Pour, Sell and Pay your debt. Now it was time for the final step.

The prophet said:

You and your sons live on the rest.

2 KINGS 4:1-7 NKJ

God not only provided enough to pay all her debts and rescue her sons from a life of slavery... there was enough left over to sustain her and her sons for life. The true meaning of the words, *"You and your sons live on the rest,"* is live and keep living on what is left after paying all your bills!

That, my friend, is **"Divine Retirement!"**

I have dedicated two chapters in this book to two different widows who needed a miracle. Each of these women were blessed when they recognized their "Powerful Point of Contact" was **Obedience** to the man of God!

Neither woman questioned or challenged the prophet, rather they obeyed fully and in the end both were blessed beyond their wildest imagination.

It is altogether possible that your, "Powerful Point of Contact," for financial independence and "Divine Retirement" is…

OBEDIENCE TO THE MAN OF GOD!

Section Three

Chapter 13
Reverse The Curse

O n that fateful day in the beautiful Garden of Eden, when the serpent successfully tempted Eve to partake of the forbidden fruit, a curse came upon the earth.

And...since all nations of men descended from that original couple, Adam and Eve, the curse has been carried down to every generation.

I want to talk to you about the terrible effects of the curse. It has caused havoc in the lives of men and women from the moment Eve partook until now.

But God provided a reverse for the curse!

Later in this chapter I will discuss in detail the reverse for the curse. Before I do, however, let's look at the various aspects of the curse and how it concerns you.

The first thing I will point out is that God never intended for His creation to experience sin, sickness, disease, heartache, poverty, pain or death. All of these common maladies are the result of the curse.

Think about what I just said, God never intended for you to be sick. When I say sick I'm talking about every form of sickness from a sniffle to heart failure, from a headache to malignant cancer and everything in between.

When God created man He made him in His own image. Man was the masterpiece of all that God made. He fashioned him to look like, think like and speak like his Creator. Inside man's bosom God placed a portion of Himself.

He created man so perfect and flawless that no sickness or disease could attach itself to him. On the day of his creation man was made to live forever.

Then disobedience reared its ugly head and man became a corrupted being. Corruption brought sickness and sickness brought death. For some the death process is slow, long and drawn out while for others it moves rapidly to claim its victim.

The curse is multi-dimensional in that it touches every facet of life, spiritually, physically, mentally and financially.

Let's talk about the curse and how it has affected each of these areas.

Adam and Eve enjoyed a boundless relationship with God. He came to the garden daily to visit with them. He was there to answer any question and to provide them with the companionship they needed.

Don't you know it was exciting to hear the voice of the Lord their God each day? Wow! God came down from the throne room on high every day to commune with the man He created.

Then disobedience, rebellion and self-gratification entered the picture and the line of communication was broken. Gone was the happy anticipation of God's next visit. All of a sudden Adam saw God, not as his benevolent protector, but as one whom he should fear.

Can you imagine the pain that would stab your heart if you came into your child's room and found him cowering in fear simply because he heard your voice? That's the reception God received when He came to the garden after sin made its entry!

Sin drove a wedge between God and man...the curse brought spiritual separation. Separation brought spiritual death... spiritual death meant eternal separation from God! Oh, what a vicious cycle!

Not only did sin bring devastation to man spiritually, it opened the door for every form of sickness and disease.

Can you believe me when I tell you that man was created so perfectly that his immune system could ward off anything trying to enter him?

Man was created with a good army marching through his veins capturing and destroying everything that wanted to do him harm. The curse opened the door for another army to enter the body of man an army of sickness, disease and physical death.

You may think I have lost my mind when I tell you that God never intended for His masterpiece to die, but it is true. Every muscle and organ, even the fiber and tissue of man was designed to constantly renew and revitalize itself from within.

The Psalmist David had this to say about the physical body:

> *For Thou didst form my inward parts; Thou didst weave me in my mother's womb. I will give thanks to Thee, for I am fearfully and wonderfully made; Wonderful are Thy works, And my soul knows it very well. My frame was not hidden from Thee, When I was made in secret, and skillfully wrought in the depths of the earth.*
>
> PSALMS 139:13-15 NAS

When God created man He didn't do it with planned obsolescence, He intended for man to live sickness and disease free for eternity!

But sin came... and with sin the curse of sickness, disease and death!

The third tragic part of the curse is what it has done to the mind of man. Do you realize that the Lord intended for man to think like God thinks?

The Lord God Jehovah didn't create man to be an ignoramus! Rather, when He fashioned the magnificent creature from the dust of the earth He placed within him an enormous reasoning capacity.

It has been proven conclusively that mankind is the only part of creation that has true reasoning capability. To put it bluntly... man is the only creature on earth that possesses the power to think.

Now I know that animal lovers will object to that statement, but it is a fact. The animal kingdom, which ranges from kitty cats to the really big cats, from elephants to mice and from lapdogs to prairie dogs, all of which are governed by natural instincts. Animals do not have reasoning power, they don't know right from wrong.

Now don't get mad at Brother Cerullo, I'm simply telling you the truth. You may want to believe that your little Fido or Cheshire-the-top-cat, can think and reason things out for themselves, but they can't.

Your dog or cat has watched you open a hundred cans of food, but if you leave a can near the can opener from now on, the animal will never get it open!

Oh, you say, their paws are not suitable for using a can opener. If you couldn't use one, you would THINK of another way to get the can open! That's because you have the ability to reason and come to conclusions.

Have you ever known of an animal coming up with an invention? Do they write poetry, songs? Do they read books or solve problems? When did you ever hear of a cat or dog that could work the simplest math equation?

I'm not casting dispersions against the animal kingdom, I'm pointing out what a marvelous creation you are. You were created with God-like qualities and abilities that no other creature has.

Sadly, the curse has also taken its toll on the human mind. What started out as pure, clean, and holy is now perverted, dirty and deranged.

The minds of men are so corrupted they have become reprobates. In every major city police are constantly looking for those whose minds have become so depraved that they are a menace to society. Not only cities, entire nations are plagued with caring for the mentally ill.

All of these maladies are the result of the curse, but thank God, He has provided a way to reverse the curse.

Sin, like a giant octopus wrapped its tentacles around the whole human race and sought to drag us all into the bottomless pit, but God through His son provided a way of escape.

The answer to sin is the blood of Jesus Christ. One of the great old hymns of the church says:

"What can wash away my sins? Nothing but the blood of Jesus! What can make me whole again? Nothing but the blood of Jesus! Oh precious is the flow that makes me white as snow, no other fount I know, nothing but the blood of Jesus."

God issued a challenge to the fallen race when He said:

Come now, and let us reason together, Says the LORD, Though your sins are like scarlet, They shall be as white as snow; Though they are red like crimson, They shall be as wool.

ISAIAH 1:18 NKJ

There is a reverse for the curse of sin if man will only avail himself of it. Jesus paid the supreme price for every sinner. Through His death we were set free from the curse of sin.

But God didn't stop there, the curse not only maligned man's spirit it brought in sickness and disease. So, once again God provided a reverse for the curse through His only begotten Son.

The prophet Isaiah looked through the divine telescope of time and witnessed a scene so horrible that it made him shudder. He saw a man tied to a whipping post being beaten mercilessly, paying the price to reverse the curse of sickness from man.

The prophet said:

But he was wounded for our transgressions, he was bruised for our iniquities: the chastisement of our peace was upon him; and with his stripes we are healed.

ISAIAH 53:5

I have no words to adequately describe the horror our Savior went through when He fulfilled the prophecy written above. This form of punishment was so severe that nine out of ten men died at the whipping post.

This is what historians tell us about the scourging Jesus suffered so that you and I could be freed from the curse of sickness and disease.

There were three ways a condemned man was beaten. The hands were placed through a leather loop that was then drawn up until only the tips of his toes touched the floor. Or his arms and hands were wrapped around a large column and tied so he couldn't move or he was laid face down on a column and tied.

Once the victim was secured, a brawny Roman soldier beat his naked back with a whip called the "cat-o-nine-tails."

The whip was so named because of the way it was made.

It was constructed of nine leather braids, twelve to eighteen inches long attached to a handle. A bone or a piece of glass or metal was woven into the end of each braid. The braids bruised the back, but the tips ripped, tore and cut the back to ribbons.

Scourging was so devastating that when an individual received forty stripes he was considered dead.

When Jesus was beaten in Pilate's judgment hall He received thirty-nine stripes. It wasn't that the executioner had mercy on Him that made him stop at thirty-nine! He did that so they could, in effect, kill Him twice.

Thirty-nine times the whip lashed across His back, each time, nine tips of bone glass or metal ripped the flesh open to the bone. Do you realize He received 351 lacerations on His precious back for you and me? That, my friend, was the price He paid to reverse the curse of sickness and disease!

Jesus Christ paid the price for our sins to be forgiven, our bodies to be healed and He made provision for our minds to be set free from the terrible, reprobate curse.

Paul, the great apostle of the New Testament declared the freedom we have in his second letter to Timothy. Notice what he said to his son in the faith:

For God has not given us a spirit of fear, but of power and of love and of a sound mind.

II TIMOTHY 1:7 NKJ

Every child of God can draw strength from this powerful verse because we are all partakers of the same covenant promises if we act in faith and walk in obedience to the will of the Father.

Let me recap the truths of this chapter that I have titled,

"Reverse the Curse."

When Adam and Eve disobeyed God they opened the entire human race to the curse. The curse subjected mankind to sin, sickness, mental oppression and poverty. None of which was in God's original plan for his magnificent creation.

Knowing that man could not by his own means break free from the curse, God took it upon Himself to provide a ransom for fallen man. The ransom demanded that Jesus Christ, the only perfect human being, die for all men! He literally took away our sin, sickness and mental oppression through His sacrifice.

If you have read this chapter carefully you have noticed that I covered the spiritual, physical and mental aspects of the curse and I've given you plenty of Scripture to substantiate the claim that Jesus paid the total price for your redemption. You have also noted that I have omitted deliverance from poverty!

Here's why!

While every other aspect of your life was included in the price Christ paid at Calvary, freedom from poverty, want, lack and shortage demands participation from you.

The Word is absolute in its teaching that you hold the key to your prosperity and financial independence.

All that is required of you to receive salvation, the infilling of the Holy Spirit, healing and mental prowess is to believe on the Lord Jesus Christ. Believing on Him is your key to every spiritual blessing. In fact, that's all you can do, because it was all paid for in His sacrifice.

Prosperity, however, demands that you do your part!

What do I mean when I say, "do your part?"

Sow good seed...in good soil!

My next statement may shock you, if it does; I pray that it shocks you to reality!

God is not obligated, nor will He obligate Himself to bless anyone who does not sow. Think with me for a moment, can a farmer reap a harvest if he plants no seed? Will his corn fields produce a bumper crop if he prays, but fails to plant any seed? Will he reap a giant harvest simply because he wants or needs one?

Obviously, the answer is no! If a farmer fails to plant when harvest time comes, all he will have in his field is weeds. No farmer in his right mind would expect to reap if he has not planted.

The same is true with you and me! Unless we plant in His Kingdom, God will not bless our finances.

Remember... the title of this chapter is "Reverse the Curse!" Part of the curse is poverty and it can... NO... it WILL be reversed when you obey the guidelines set forth in the Word.

Are you ready to receive your "Powerful Point of Contact," for financial freedom? Are you ready to reverse the curse from your life and begin to live in God's realm of abundance?

If you will accept the Word for what it says and act upon it, you will move from want to plenty.

Are you really ready?

Let this truth sink deep in your spirit! This is not the word of Morris Cerullo, it is not the promise of some fraternal order or a church doctrine, this is the eternal Word of God:

Will a man rob God? Yet you have robbed Me! But you say, In what way have we robbed You? In tithes and offerings. You are cursed with a curse, For you have robbed Me, Even this whole nation. Bring all the tithes into the storehouse, That there may be food in My house, And try Me now in this, Says the LORD of hosts, If I will not open for you the windows of heaven And pour out for you such blessing That there will not be room enough to receive it. And I will rebuke the

devourer for your sakes, So that he will not destroy the
fruit of your ground, Nor shall the vine fail to bear fruit
for you in the field, Says the LORD of hosts; And all
nations will call you blessed, For you will be a delightful
land, Says the LORD of hosts.

MALACHI 3:8-12 NKJ

Did you see what God said? *"You are cursed with a curse!"*
Remember, this chapter is dedicated to "reversing the curse,"
so let's pay attention to what He said to do. *"Bring all the*
tithes into the storehouse!"

I am amazed at how simple God made it for you and me
to break the chains of darkness and reverse the curse.
Through the Prophet Malachi He said, "pay tithes and give
offerings!" Nothing more and nothing less is expected of you
and me. Notice what He said He will do when we obey:

...try Me now in this, Says the LORD of hosts, If I will not
open for you the windows of heaven And pour out for you such
blessing That there will not be room enough to receive it. And
I will rebuke the devourer for your sakes, So that he will not
destroy the fruit of your ground, Nor shall the vine fail to bear
fruit for you in the field.

It may surprise you to know that only once in the entire
Bible are we challenged to "try" God. That one time is what
you have just read. It is in regards to your "reversing the
curse" of poverty, want, lack and penury.

You can literally change your destiny, move away from
poverty, lack and want and enter into God's abundance by
paying your tithes and giving offerings.

I am revealing a "Powerful Point of Contact" to you that
will release you from the curse of not having enough money
to live a prosperous life.

I pray that you will take hold of this "Powerful Point of
Contact," right now. You do it by sowing into good,
soul-winning soil.

Every smart farmer knows that he must sow good seed in good soil to reap a bountiful harvest – you too must sow your money in a good soul-winning ministry to reap the abundance God has planned for you.

"Reverse the curse" from your life today by paying your tithes and giving offerings to win the lost! This is your

"Powerful Point of Contact!"

Section Three

Conclusion

One of the greatest promises in the Word of God regarding prosperity is found in Paul's second letter to the Corinthians:

Now He who supplies seed to the sower and bread for food, will supply and multiply your seed for sowing and increase the harvest of your righteousness; you will be enriched in everything for all liberality, which through us is producing thanksgiving to God.

II CORINTHIANS 9:10-11 NAS

Did you notice the apostle's exact words? *"He who supplies seed to the sower."*

Many people find it amazing this doesn't say God supplies seed to the needy. That would seem to be the most likely group to supply seed to.

And He didn't say to the wishers! Imagine how many takers He would have had if wishers were being supplied seed. Heaven knows seed would be rotting on every corner if God wasted it on wishers.

Paul didn't say to the promisers! If God supplied seed to everyone who promised to plant it, there would be bags of seed in almost every garage in America.

The promise was not given to the hopeful! Hope is wonderful, but it doesn't meet God's criteria for Him to supply seed. The Bible says, *"And now abide faith, hope, love, these three..."* I Corinthians 13:13 NKJ

Hope is one of the three great attributes of God that He shares with His children and it is a powerful force, but God does not provide seed for the hopeful.

The apostle said, "God supplies seed to the sowers!"

THINK ABOUT IT...TO THE SOWERS!

Let this truth sink deep into your spirit! Prosperity is not automatic. You do not become rich or financially independent simply because you are a child of God...

You must make it happen!

I am going to challenge you to do something right now that will alter your destiny, your future, the way you think and the way you live.

I have prepared a special *"Blessing Pact Prayer Form and Envelope"* especially for you. Take it in your hands now and write out these three things:

1. Your physical need!

2. Your spiritual need!

3. Your financial need!

Now I challenge you to open the envelope and enclose your needs and the greatest seed offering you possibly can to help me win the lost to Christ and to build God an army!

As you obey the prophet you are giving your seed a name and you are setting your harvest in motion.

Remember...

Nothing is automatic...you must make it happen!

Section Four
Introduction

Each section of this book is written to help you establish your own "Powerful Point of Contact" and receive miracles from God. The concluding section is the most important of all, because it unveils the central theme of the Word of God.

Some may want to read this section on bended knees as an act of humility to God the Father for giving His only begotten Son to save us from our sins. And to the Lord Jesus Christ for enduring the most excruciating death known to man! And to the sweet Holy Spirit Who daily draws us back to the Cross, from whence our salvation so freely flows.

Heaven spreads wide its arms to welcome anyone and everyone from the four corners of the earth who finds refuge from their sins in the Cross.

There is a cleansing stream that washes away every stain from the penitent who come to the portals of glory through the Cross. But entry into the Celestial is denied to anyone who tries to enter by any other way.

May the words of this beautiful old hymn resonate in your heart as you read this concluding section:

Near the Cross

Jesus keep me near the Cross, There a precious fountain;Free to all a healing stream, Flows from Calvary's Mountain. In the Cross, In the Cross, Be my glory ever; Till my raptured soul shall find; Peace beyond the river!

Section Four

Chapter 14

The Cross

Heaven is the ultimate goal of every man, woman and child and...not just those of the Christian Faith!

I have discussed eternity with Jews, Buddhists, Moslems, Hindus and people from many other religions and they all want to go to the place of eternal rest whether they call it paradise, utopia or any of a hundred other names.

Even those who claim to be atheists,
when faced with death, want to go to heaven!

What is the criterion for getting into heaven? Is it based on how good a person is? If a man or woman believes strongly enough in their religion will he or she be welcomed into the place of celestial glory?

What if a person's god is the moon? What about those who worship nature? Will the moon or Mother Nature escort them into paradise and grant eternal favor to them? Will the sun leave its place in the sky to lead its loyal followers through the gates of splendor?

Surely the sun worshippers are not so stupid as to think that they could draw near to their god. If they do, they will quickly discover that their bliss has turned to blisters.

Tree huggers and other nature worshippers along with all

the "moon babies" will also find out that simply believing in "something" does not open heaven's portals.

So...what does it take to get into the Celestial City called Heaven?

Jesus Christ answered that question two thousand years ago. He said:

> *Let not your heart be troubled; you believe in God, believe also in Me. In My Father's house are many mansions; if it were not so, I would have told you. I go to prepare a place for you. And if I go and prepare a place for you, I will come again and receive you to Myself; that where I am, there you may be also. And where I go you know, and the way you know. Thomas said to Him, Lord, we do not know where You are going, and how can we know the way? Jesus said to him, I am the way, the truth, and the life. No one comes to the Father except through Me.*
>
> JOHN 14:1-6 NKJ

In this compilation of verses Jesus not only talked about Heaven in the most positive manner, but He also laid down the guidelines for getting there.

Let's analyze His dialog with the disciples!

In His opening statement Jesus is encouraging His followers to cement their faith in the Father and in Him. This conversation was to forewarn them of His impending crucifixion.

He wanted the disciples to understand that the purpose for His coming to earth was not to establish an earthly kingdom for the Jewish race, but to prepare men and women of all races for eternity.

When Jesus said, *"Let not your heart be troubled; you believe in God, believe also in Me,"* He was telling them not to lose hope when the hour of temptation came. He was setting the stage for the most crucial hour the earth had ever witnessed.

Christ knew that He was destined to die for the sins of the world. He also knew that His disciples had no comprehension that such a tremendous sacrifice was necessary and their faith would be severely tested when He was arrested, condemned and crucified.

After telling them of his death He revealed one of the great truths of the Word. Notice what He said, *"In My Father's house are many mansions; if it were not so, I would have told you."*

Wanting to make light of this wonderful promise, a scoffer said to me, "Who ever heard of someone having mansions in their house?" My answer, "You just haven't seen my Father's house!"

Several years ago someone wrote a song entitled, "Lord Build Me a Cabin in the Corner of Glory Land." When I heard it, I said, that's not my song! I don't want a cabin in the corner, I want a palatial mansion on the corner of Glory Boulevard and Hallelujah Street.

I will never settle for a cabin when the architect of the universe promised: *"I go to prepare a place for you."* Think about it, He has prepared a mansion for you and me and it has our names above the doors!

No cabins, no shanty shacks, no slums or ghettos, just mansions lining every golden street in a city that's 1500 miles cube. You read that correctly, the city is not just square it's cube! John the Revelator said:

> *And the city is laid out as a square, and its length is as great as the width; and he measured the city with the rod, fifteen hundred miles;* ***its length and width and height are equal.***
>
> REVELATION 21:16 NAS

Let me explain the size of the Holy City to you in terms

that are easy to grasp!

If you start at San Diego and go East 1500 miles you will go about fifty miles past Houston, Texas. Turn left and go 1500 miles North. This will take you above the United States border into Canada. Turn left again and go 1500 miles West into the Province of British Colombia. Turn south and when you get back to San Diego you will have made a journey of about the size of the ground floor of the Heavenly City.

I emphasize the statement, "the ground floor," because, the height of this magnificent city is the same as the length and width! Do you realize your mansion could be a mile high and there would be room for 1500 more, equally as tall, stacked above it?

This city is so immense that if you spend twenty four hours on each square mile you will not cover the ground floor in 10,000 years. Now multiply that by 1500, providing there is a mile between floors.

As you can tell, I am enamored with the thought of Heaven. It reminds me of an old spiritual they used to sing in the South:

"Heaven, is better than this, oh my what joy what bliss; Walking on streets of solid gold, living in a land where we'll never grow old; Heaven, is better than this, oh my what joy what bliss; I love the saints and the preachers too, but Heaven is better than this!"

I could go on and on talking about the glories of that wonderful place Jesus has gone to prepare for you and me. But this chapter isn't about Heaven, rather, who is going and how we can get there!

Too many people equate getting to Heaven with getting to cities on earth. A man said to a minister friend of mine, "there are many roads leading into Dallas, Texas, and it must be the same with Heaven." My friend answered, "If Dallas is as far as you want to go then you can take any road you choose, but if you want to go to Heaven, there is only one way!"

That statement may not set well with folks who want to be politically correct. "After all," they say, "we must be tolerant with all religions, we must not be narrow minded."

When I hear people, especially ministers say that we must accept every religion, because they all have their good points, it makes me sick at my stomach. If that is true, then Jesus Christ died in vain and the Bible is a farce!

Either Jesus is Who He says He is or He is the worst charlatan the world has ever seen! I choose to believe He is the "Only Begotten Son of God and every word He spoke, to be the absolute, eternal, everlasting Truth.

Continuing the Lord's dialogue with His disciples, after promising a glorious place in Heaven, Jesus said:

> *And if I go and prepare a place for you, I will come again and receive you to Myself; that where I am, there you may be also. And where I go you know, and the way you know. Thomas said to Him, Lord, we do not know where You are going, and how can we know the way? Jesus said to him, I am the way, the truth, and the life. No one comes to the Father except through Me.*

Had Jesus considered the "politically correct" way to answer him when Thomas said, *"Lord, we do not know where You are going, and how can we know the way?"* He would have said, "I am one of the many ways, one of the many truths and one of the many lives," but He didn't! Jesus said: *"I am the way, the truth, and the life. No one comes to the Father except through Me."*

Let this dynamic Truth sink deep into your spirit!

181

Jesus said: *"I am THE way, THE truth, and THE life."* Not a way or a truth or a life… He said I am "THE," singular, the One and Only WAY…TRUTH…LIFE!

Then Christ made the most conclusive statement ever to dispel the myth that simply believing in something is all it takes to get to Heaven. He said: *"No one comes to the Father except through Me."*

Some religious people think Jesus was being bigoted when He made this statement, but that's because they don't want to accept Him as the Savior of the world.

Since the beginning of time Mankind has tried to make God fit into his foolish mold. That's why men throughout the ages have fashioned gods of wood, metal and stone. But God cannot be made to conform to man's imagination. God is God and man must be conformed into His image.

Your family, your husband or your wife, your children and your grandchildren, your parents and all your relatives must be made to realize that there is only one way to Heaven.

It is not enough to simply "get religion!" It is not enough to be good and treat others right!

Let me remind you of Christ's words to a religious man:

> *There was a man of the Pharisees named Nicodemus, a ruler of the Jews. This man came to Jesus by night and said to Him, Rabbi, we know that You are a teacher come from God; for no one can do these signs that You do unless God is with him. Jesus answered and said to him, Most assuredly, I say to you, unless one is born again, he cannot see the kingdom of God.*
>
> JOHN 3:1-4 NKJ

Did you notice how Jesus cut through the religious jargon?

The Jewish ruler could have argued for hours over the

smallest "jot or tittle," (those are accent marks in the Hebrew language) had Jesus allowed him to, but He didn't. The Lord went directly to the heart of the matter and told him, "religion just won't cut it, if you are going to see the kingdom of God, you must be born again!"

There are no shortcuts! No secondary choices, no alternate routes! Jesus is **THE** way, **THE** truth and **THE** life. No one comes to the Father except through Him.

Many people's perception of God is that He is an angry old man with a long white beard, a scowl on His face and He carries a big stick to smite anyone who does not please Him. And… they think of Christ as the kind, loving Intercessor who stands before the throne pleading with the Father not to punish us.

If men, women and children only knew how much God loves them and the price He paid for their redemption!

Let's talk about His great love!

The Bible says:

For God so loved the world, that he gave his only begotten Son, that whosoever believeth in him should not perish, but have everlasting life.

JOHN 3:16

I want you to pay special attention to the first six words of this wonderful verse, *"For God so loved the world."*

My concept of God, as a young Jewish boy growing up in the harsh environment of an Orthodox Jewish Orphanage, was that He was as mean as the overbearing Rabbi and his wife. Since the man and woman who beat me and sent me to bed hungry represented Him, I could only imagine that He was like them.

I will never forget the first time I realized that God really is a God of love. I read these words over and over again *"For God so loved the world, For God so loved the world, For God so loved the world."* When those words finally reached my inner being I saw God in a totally different light.

No longer did I think of Him as an angry God who was out to get me, but as a true loving Father who always had my best interest at heart. At last, I could read the words of the prophet and believe that He really did love me and want to bless me.

> *For I know the plans I have for you, declares the LORD, plans to prosper you and not to harm you, plans to give you hope and a future.*
>
> JEREMIAH 29:11-12 NIV

When God gave His Son, Jesus, to be the sacrificial Lamb He wanted all men to know His true nature. Notice the exact wording of the next verse.

> *For God sent not his Son into the world to condemn the world; but that the world through him might be saved.*
>
> JOHN 3:17

Friend, this is still talking about the great love of God. True, it was Jesus who died for our sins, but it was the love of the Father that compelled Christ to give His life as a ransom for us.

Even before sin entered the human race and man fell from his high estate, God devised the plan of salvation.

The Word declares in Revelation 13:8, that Jesus was slain from the foundation of the earth. What that means is that before Eve was deceived and Adam disobeyed God's command, because the Lord knew that man would sin, He provided the atonement.

In providing a cure, a covering, a sacrifice for sin God also established a universal "Point of Contact" for every man, woman and child. This "Powerful Point of Contact" is the Cross!

Neither time nor eternity will ever replace the importance of the Cross!

From the lips of the crucified One we have these words:

And I, if I be lifted up from the earth, will draw all men unto me. This he said, signifying what death he should die.

JOHN 12:32-33

Too many people quote the first of those two verses and take it completely out of text. I've heard dozens of preachers repeat the Lord's words, *"And I, if I be lifted up from the earth, will draw all men unto me."* and they finish by saying, so let's lift Him up.

Jesus was not talking about being exalted... He was declaring to His followers that He was going to be nailed to the Cross.

Let the words of the Lord sink deep into your spirit. When He said, *"And I, if I be lifted up from the earth,"* He was talking about the Cross!

In another place Jesus said:

... as Moses lifted up the serpent in the wilderness, even so must the Son of Man be lifted up, that whoever believes in Him should not perish but have eternal life.

JOHN 3:14-15 NKJ

Did the words, *"even so must the Son of Man be lifted up,"* strike a familiar cord in your heart? The "lifting up" was fulfilled when Jesus was led outside the city of Jerusalem to the lonely hill called Golgotha... there He was crucified. It was there that He died for you and me.

I am reminded of a stanza to one of the great anthems of the Church:

"To the old rugged Cross I will ever be true, Its shame and reproach gladly bear; Till He calls me some day, to my home far away, Where His glory forever I'll share. So, I'll cherish the old rugged Cross, Till my trophies at last I lay down; I will cling to the old rugged Cross, And exchange it some day for a crown."

Since the beginning of time there has never been nor will there ever be a "Point of Contact" more powerful, more universal or more accessible to every living soul than the CROSS.

When Jesus said, *"And I, if I be lifted up from the earth, will draw all men unto me,"* He was saying, every man, woman, boy and girl who wants to go to Heaven must come by the way of the Cross.

More than fifty-five years ago God transported me to Heaven and showed me the wonders of our eternal home.

Then He pulled back the curtain of time and let me gaze in horror at the souls in hell, surrounded by the flames of the Lake of Fire. God let me know that the only way to avoid going to that terrible place of torment is to come through the CROSS to Him.

I realized on that day that I must forget about my plans to be an attorney and go to the ends of the earth with the message of the crucified Savior. I can still hear the cries of the damned. In my mind's eye I can still see the flames of the lake of fire.

After all these years the passion for the lost still burns in my heart. My number one goal is to plunder hell and populate Heaven! I want all men everywhere to know the way of the Cross leads home!

Look at the words of Paul the apostle:

For the preaching of the cross is to them that perish foolishness; but unto us which are saved it is the power of God.

I CORINTHIANS 1:18

If the Apostle Paul were writing this book, at this juncture he would emphasize this truth... the Cross is the most "Powerful Point of Contact" in the universe. It is the one central truth that can bankrupt hell and flood the golden streets with righteous souls.

Oh yes, God gave Heaven's best to redeem fallen man from the curse of sin and He made the plan of salvation so easy that even a fool should not miss it.

Hear the words of the Crucified One saying, *"And I, if I be lifted up from the earth, will draw all men unto me, This he said, signifying what death he should die!"*

When He was lifted up, suspended between Heaven and earth on the Cross, with one hand He reached the throne room on high and touched the Father. With His other hand He reached down to fallen man. In His death on the Cross He paid the price for every lost soul. Nothing more was needed, redemption's plan was complete forevermore.

The Cross became the doorway through which every man, woman and child must pass to get into Heaven. There is no other road, no other path... the Cross literally is ... the only way home!

When Moses lifted up the serpent in the wilderness he said to the people who had been bitten by the fiery serpents, "Look and live!" And whoever looked was healed of the snake's poison.

In like manner, I say to everyone who has fallen prey to the forces of darkness, "Look to Him who was nailed to the old rugged Cross!" It was not the pieces of wood that bought your redemption, but Christ who died for your sins.

Hear His words one more time, *"And I, if I be lifted up from the earth, will draw all men unto me, This he said, signifying what death he should die!"*

The most "Powerful Point of Contact" in all the universe is the Cross!

Section Four

Conclusion

This is by no stretch of the imagination a complete study of the Cross. Thousands of pages have been written on the subject, yet without fail, when the authors have finished they have known that there is more left unsaid than the pens of man can ever write.

The Cross, is for you, your children, your spouse, your friends and your loved ones. Because of it, hope springs eternally in the heart of the believer.

Heaven awaits those who come to its gates through the Cross. For every searching soul the way of the Cross, leads home!

Friend, Right Now reach out to the cross of Calvary - Embrace Jesus as your Lord and Saviour - Check the box on the: Blessing Pact Prayer Envelope. Envelope - As an act of your Point of Contact For the Salvation of your soul God Bless you.

Brother Cerullo

There is a greater anointing upon me now than ever before to pray for your needs.

Never before, in my more than 56 years of frontline ministry have I carried a deeper burden for the Body of Christ than I do now.

I have prayed, fasted, interceded, agonized and fought spiritual warfare against satanic powers...

...and God gave me a vision!

God said..."Place the needs of my people upon the altar before My Presence...Jesus is praying for all their needs to be met!"

A vision of Jesus Christ, our Great High Priest, praying for all your needs.

God said, *"Place the needs of my people upon the altar before My Presence. Jesus is praying for all their needs to be met."*

Every need, every disease, every family problem, every circumstance...God wants me to lift your need for Jesus to pray for you. Do not delay. Write all your needs on the following page and mail it to me today!

For prayer 24 hours a day, 7 days a week, call:

1-858-HELPLINE
435-7546

Brother Cerullo,

Please place these requests on the Miracle Prayer Altar and pray for these needs:

_____

_____

_____

_____

_____

q   Enclosed is my love gift of $(£)_____ to help you win souls and to support this worldwide ministry.

q   Please tell me how I can become a God's Victorious Army member...to help you reach the nations of the world, and receive even more anointed teaching on a monthly basis!

Name _____

Address _____

City _____ State or Province _____

Postal Code _____ Phone Number (____)_____

E-mail_____

Fax _____

Mail today to:

MORRIS CERULLO WORLD EVANGELISM

San Diego: PO. Box 85277 • San Diego, CA 92186

Canada: PO. Box 3600 • Concord, Ontario L4K 1B6

U.K.: PO. Box 277 • Hemel Hempstead, Herts HP2 7DH

Web site: www.mcwe.com • **E-mail:** morriscerullo@mcwe.com

For prayer 24 hours a day, 7 days a week, call: **1-858-HELPLINE**
435-7546

HELPLINE FAX: 1-858-427-0555

EMAIL: helpline @mcwe.com

Miracles Happen When Someone Cares...And We Care What Happens To You!

Call if you need healing, restoration in your marriage, financial breakthrough, deliverance from alcohol, drugs or other addictions,

World Prayer Center

- Prayer Help Line

- Trained, anointed intercessors. Only qualified, trained intercessors will be on the phone lines.

YOUR PHONE IS YOUR POINT OF CONTACT!

- Non-denominational: We encourage Catholic, Protestants, Jews, people of all faiths to call

You Never Have To Face Your Circumstances Alone!

There is no distance in prayer!

Our trained intercessors are ready to pray and believe God for the miracle you need!

Call the 24 hours a day, 7 days a week Morris Cerullo Prayer Help Line

1-858-HELPLINE

Helpline@mcwe.com
Fax: 858-427-0555

435-7546

192